PRACTICAL ELECTIONS ADM

Practical Elections Administration

David Monks

Chief Executive
Huntingdonshire District Council

Shaw & Sons

Shaw's
Since 1750

Published by
Shaw & Sons Limited
Shaway House
21 Bourne Park
Bourne Road
Crayford
Kent DA1 4BZ

www.shaws.co.uk

Published January 2008

ISBN 978 0 7219 1740 5

A CIP catalogue record for this book is available from the British Library

DISCLAIMER
Whilst every care has been taken in the preparation of this book, neither
the author, the Society of Local Authority Chief Executives nor Shaw & Sons
Limited can accept liability for inaccuracies in, errors in or omissions from the
text or the use thereof.

Printed in Great Britain by
Antony Rowe Limited, Chippenham

CONTENTS

Contents

THE AUTHOR

David Monks is Chief Executive of Huntingdonshire District Council and Chairman of the SOLACE Electoral Matters Panel. He has been a Returning Officer for over 20 years (including being the Eastern Regional Returning Officer for the 1999 and 2004 European Parliamentary Elections) and is a regular writer and speaker on electoral topics.

INTRODUCTION

"Running Elections is now a significantly different process from that delivered five or so years ago. It is far from a routine administrative exercise" Electoral Commission Report on Postal Voting, July 2007

The administration of elections is not straightforward and, regrettably, is often a process attended by a variety of difficulties. This somewhat negative starting point applies to all types of election, ranging from contests for overall parliamentary control at Westminster to the less publicised Parish Council by-election.

Much has been said in very recent years about our out-dated Victorian electoral system and its unsuitability for the 21st Century. Reform always seems to be piecemeal – however loudly lauded by the Government – and we still have not managed to consolidate electoral legislation. The latest Electoral Administration Act of 2006 (and consequent regulations) simply makes amendments to earlier provisions.

Indeed, the value and practical effectiveness of those changes caused tremendous problems at the 2007 local elections. The AEA, in publishing its first ever post-election report, wrote that "these were the most difficult set of elections to administer within living memory". Their report describes "the inappropriate approach by Government to funding and resources for electoral services and how the determination to introduce new measures to combat fraud without proper and rigorous testing almost brought the service to its knees."

It is against that unhappy background that this book appears. Its purpose is clear – to attempt to dispel some dissatisfaction and to enable elections to be run in a smoother fashion by concentrating on some of the tricky, practical details. Whatever the gaps and vagaries of electoral legislation and law (there is no shortage of case law), the Returning Officer and Electoral Administrator must carry out the process to the best of their ability and, above all, achieve a result. Thus, this text seeks to focus on moving the process on and practical resolutions of issues (note: the words "solutions to problems" are deliberately not used in this sentence).

Accordingly, this publication is not a complete commentary on all electoral provisions and practice; for that see other books such as *Schofield's Election Law*.

By means of self-contained chapters, it looks at some of the key stages in the process and recounts actions taken, often by way of anecdote. That is not to say these actions are unchallengeable or, indeed, monopolise wit, wisdom and truth but, frequently from adversity, achieve a satisfactory outcome.

There is another reason for the production of this humble monograph. Like many areas of the public sector, there is an "oral tradition" (in the Old Testament sense) within electoral practice that it would be beneficial to record. The writer has spoken at many conferences and workshops, frequently encountering sound advice that is neither documented nor published elsewhere. Whilst accepting that not all contributions at these events fall into that category, there are many examples of good practice, innovative thinking and downright resilience that could benefit many others. This text seeks to repair those omissions.

It is hoped the selections that follow will benefit those charged with the onerous burden of "delivering democracy" in this country. Needless to say, thanks are due to a number of people for their help and support throughout – Crispin Williams of Shaws, Andrea Lucken for her excellent work on the text, David Cowan for his comments on Chapter 7, John Turner and the AEA for their 2007 Report, numerous SOLACE colleagues for their submissions of private reports and anecdotes, and too many others to mention individually from the small world of the electoral family.

David Monks
Huntingdon, Autumn 2007

Chapter 1

RETURNING OFFICERS

"Returning Officers have to keep the lifeblood of modern democracy flowing and make sure that the gateway to power and influence is properly serviced. The bare fact put, perhaps in somewhat dramatic language, reveals an essential truth, namely, that the gatekeepers can be attacked both in the way they control the approach to the gate and after someone has been let through the gate"
Tim Straker QC speaking at an Elections Conference

Appointments and associated process

Most Chief Executives (but not all) of local authorities are automatically – as a matter of custom and practice – designated as Returning Officers for all local and parliamentary elections. There has been no recent survey by, say, either the Electoral Commission or SOLACE as to how many Chief Executives are *not* Returning Officers, but the number must be small: about 10% or less? For better or worse, there is an inevitability about this process which, more frequently in the 21st Century, can cause serious problems and challenges to Returning Officers, especially those who have had virtually no contact with the electoral process in their earlier career.

At places where the Chief Executive is not Returning Officer, the usual appointee is the Council's Director of Administration, City Solicitor/ Borough Solicitor, etc. Clearly, local circumstances prevail in these cases, as they do in a number of other authorities where the Elections Manager/Administrator is the Returning Officer.

To the outsider (and even some on the inside such as newly elected members) the position is further complicated by the appointment of the Electoral Registration Officer. Again the general, but not universal, rule is that this is also the Chief Executive and Returning Officer.

However, over the years, local government has often managed to appoint different personages to these roles, driven by factors totally unconnected with rational thought and clarity, let alone accountability and effective electoral administration. No doubt such actions were well meaning in the context of their contemporary circumstances, but people do move on and some local authorities simply perpetuate the same arrangements. This is not with malice aforethought but simply lacking attention to detail and organisational inertia.

There are other national and historical factors that cause even more confusion. Thus, the Lord Mayor/Mayor/Chairman in certain old Boroughs/Cities as well as the High Sheriff in the Shires is actually styled the Returning Officer for Westminster parliamentary elections. They have only two ceremonial powers – to receive the writ and read out the result at the count. Both powers have to be actively claimed once a General Election is called and notified to the Acting Returning Officer (as the Chief Executive or whoever at the Council is Returning Officer) is now styled; outside these two claimable powers, the actual conduct of the election is entirely a matter for the Acting Returning Officer and his/her staff.

The wisdom, logic and usefulness of these archaic provisions in the modern world is difficult to see, if indeed at all visible. The reasons for this old-fashioned custom are long lost in the mists of medieval time (Simon de Montfort "returning" Knights of the Shires) but still followed today. Whilst, in certain fields of work, there may be a certain charm in retaining historical custom and, moreover, some worthwhileness in being reminded of our great traditions in this country, this can hardly apply to effective, modern electoral administration. The absurdity of these old rules was pressed on the Home Office (as the then Government Department responsible for elections) some 20 to 30 years ago and a number of senior Returning Officers felt at that time the case for reform was unchallengeable. This view was not shared by the Shrivalty Society (as representing High Sheriffs) who, with their strong connections at high levels, soon killed off any proposals for change. Nevertheless, in future, if there is to be any serious thought given to modernising our electoral system, making it "fit for purpose" in today's world, then this issue should be revisited by both the Government and the Electoral Commission. In the meantime, however, contact should be maintained by Electoral Administrators with Under Sheriffs (usually local solicitors) in the speculative period running up to a General Election so that clear arrangements can be made if the High Sheriff wants to read the result at your count (dealing with the writ is not universally popular).

None of the foregoing is improved by another complicating national and legislative factor, namely the number of other appointment titles the Returning Officer can hold: Counting Officer at Referendums, Regional Returning Officer for the European Parliamentary Elections, the ballot holder for a Business Improvement District (BID) ballot, etc. In all, there are some 15 different types of elections or polls in England and Wales and, therefore, changes of title do occur according to the election/poll taking place.

Even the most generous spirited could only describe the foregoing as a complete and utter mess, desperately in need of rationalisation and reform. Nevertheless, those in local authorities seem to manage to make a more than workable attempt to apply these provisions to various situations and, considering the muddled circumstances, produce surprisingly impressive results! The best practical advice to achieve such results is for the newly appointed Returning Officer to be clear about the terms of his/her various appointments. Practice invariably differs from local authority to local authority but good starting points are the Chief Executive contract of employment and the Council's constitution. The former should contain something along the lines that the Chief Executive as, say, District Chief Executive of an English Local Authority, is Local Returning Officer for European Elections, Acting Returning Officer for a parliamentary, Returning Officer for district and parish elections (though one authority, for a good number of years, appointed separate Returning Officers for parliamentary and local elections). Some similar wording should appear in the Council's constitution (scheme of delegations/appointment section) specifically identifying the postholder as responsible for the conduct of these "and all other elections and polls" as a sweeping-up provision.

Other authorities make specific appointments by name at Council meetings when there is a change of postholder or the Chief Executive is, sadly, suspended or absent through illness. Some of these are often made at short notice in the weeks running up to a May election! Again, to be clear, these are appointments that the local authority can and do make. However, if a Returning Officer wishes to appoint a Deputy Returning Officer, this is an entirely personal appointment made by the Returning Officer and not by the local authority. The Returning Officer can delegate all or some of his responsibilities to a deputy (or more usually deputies) for a particular election – deputy appointments that run on from year to year are not typical. Thus, in the electoral world people speak of "full powers deputies" who can carry out all the duties of the Returning Officer. Some are entrusted only with more limited responsibilities – adjudication upon nominations is a fairly typical example. It is a wise practice to appoint several deputies for all elections as Returning Officers suffer from illnesses or absences from work due to family problems like any other member of staff. Moreover, it also helps to share the workload at particularly busy periods of the elections process – comparatively simple tasks like signing off results declarations can be sped up if handled by two or three people in a hall with numerous counts involving 20 or 30 wards or parishes.

An awkward practical issue that arose in early 2007 concerned a Chief Executive/Returning Officer who had been suspended by his authority after a difficult few months and a very tense relationship with the Leader. But, who would conduct the local elections in May? No deputies had been appointed by the Chief Executive (he was suspended and not present at the office) and the Council's majority group certainly did not wish to recall him for this task alone. There was some confusion as to whether his suspension was as Chief Executive only and not covering the Returning Officer post; could he appoint deputies whilst under suspension? Several senior Returning Officers were consulted privately and, eventually, the Council were advised to convene a special meeting to appoint another chief officer as Returning Officer for this election, revoking the appointment of the suspended postholder. It was considered too risky to have a suspended officer carrying out executive tasks whilst under suspension (albeit that the Returning Officer is a personal appointment) and could incur problems if a challenge was made to the result. It would also raise questions over the insurance policy; would the insurers cover a suspended officer (probably not) and this could lead to doubts over the cover extant for actions in appointing deputies of the same person whilst suspended.

But why is the appointment issue so significant? Some Chief Executives simply take the view that they always run elections in their authorities whatever circumstances arise – the members expect this, the staff expect this too, as do candidates, agents, press, police, etc. No one else is responsible for this work and to gainsay otherwise with technicalities and differing titles is simply lawyers' pedantry. However, this is to ignore a key practical point – the ever-complex issue of insurance. This will be dealt with later in some detail but, if you are not properly appointed, insurance companies can easily take the view that you are not covered by their policy which provides cover for the proper Returning Officer (or whoever) for a particular election, not someone who simply assumes the role by virtue of expectation of others and long-standing practice. It is always worthwhile checking the details of this as a number of authorities have variations on the theme of the already tricky concept of insurance. Make sure it covers you in whatever capacity you are acting whilst running a particular election. This is a personal responsibility (not the Council's) and it is simply essential to be properly covered, as we shall see later in Chapter 11.

Resources and Returning Officers

At whatever level the Returning Officer is appointed in the authority (if not at Chief Executive level), it is important that he/she has a strong voice as an advocate for the electoral/registration process. This is a particularly key point in the contentious issue of resource allocation. As burdens on the public purse increase, it is vitally important that the electoral and electoral registration processes are not starved of either finance or manpower in seeking to respond to an ever-demanding public, as well as keeping up to date with, and implementing, legislative changes. Ever-pressurised resources are being strained at both national and local levels to meet these demands and, frankly, there will always be insufficient resource. Again, at local level, the electoral/registration process, although seen as important by elected members, can never be as attention-grabbing as the other services that local authorities deliver – social services, housing, the environment, benefits, etc.... To many members, the compiling of the register is simply a back office process of producing a list of names and surely can receive inferior (if not reduced) funding when compared with some other sharp end, front line services? This is where the strong officer is needed, to remind members as they pore over the draft budgets that an accurate and comprehensive register is the basis of successfully running an election (at both national and local levels) otherwise the chances increase that the authority (and Returning Officer) will be making national media headlines over fraud and/or failures of the process. There can be no guarantee that even with an accurate register you will avoid fraud or other problems, but an inaccurate and patchy register will inevitably lead to problems downstream in the process. Someone appointed at a lowish level in the organisation will have difficulties in communicating these ideas to decision makers, either lacking contacts (or experience in dealing with them) or having to rely on another to make the case, who probably has many other similar demands for more resources. Such is life in modern local government and it is likely to continue; a previous Chief Executive of the Audit Commission said a few years ago that funding in the public sector is basically about rationing and will never be able to respond fully to all the demands.

The modern Chief Executive as Returning Officer

As we have noted above, an increasing number of appointees to the Chief Executive/Returning Officer position have no direct (or indirect) experience of electoral work before they take up the reins of their new job. This is far from fatal and there are always opportunities for learning and personal development. It is certainly not necessary to be an expert constitutional lawyer to be a successful Returning Officer, but this is the view that many new appointees hold from when they start considering the voluminous and unco-ordinated legislation in this field of work. The 19th Century legislation – and that continuing style to the present day – is highly off-putting and inaccessible to those who come from different professional backgrounds, especially if their provenance is outside local government. The legislation envisages the old-style 19th Century Town Clerk who is a master of the "command-control" school of management. The legislation is written in a very directive way "...the Returning officer will do this or that..." "...his [these people were, without exception, males!] staff will lock postal vote ballot boxes" etc. The process and timetable of an election is very rigorous and unforgiving so it is probably harsh to criticise in this way for the legislation must be *de rigueur* of a highly prescriptive nature. However, the problem is that it does not really fit in with the working pattern of a modern local authority Chief Executive. "Command-Control" is largely rejected as a general management method and contemporary Chief Executives focus on partnership working, building/developing officer teams, working closely with elected members on policies and strategies, responding to Central Government initiatives, etc. To say to a Chief Executive in the 21st Century that he/she has a formal power to demand of his/her authority sufficient staff to carry out electoral duties and the ability to requisition certain buildings for the same purpose, is simply to invite a puzzled stare. Of all the techniques to employ in working in a political environment (often highly charged too), threats are the least likely to succeed, especially when backed with statutory force. Thus, the problem is that the legislation (much in need of modification and simplification) is out of kilter with the modern Chief Executive role. Many new Chief Executives (and some of more lengthy experience) speak quite openly, saying they do *not* want to be Returning Officers. They have a huge number of pressures and this is now such a niche role it simply does not fit in with the format of their other work.

And to be an effective Returning Officer? A good starting point is to see the role as an overall managerial one, leading a team in a co-ordinated project to deliver results. There is so much technical detail in electoral law and procedure that the Returning Officer (even experienced lawyers) cannot know everything and must rely on other staff – generally electoral administrators who carry out all the detailed work. Many of the latter complain quite fairly and genuinely that their Chief Executive/Returning Officer shows little interest in the process, and this is quite indefensible; the Chief Executive must be part of the team in an active way. Another good way to demonstrate this is to take the lead in dealing with the media and speak out as Returning Officer if there are stories about the election in the local press. The national press tend now to show greater interest in electoral stories, mainly involving fraud and problems with the process. We shall consider the topic of dealing with the media later in Chapter 7.

Chapter 2

POLLING STATIONS

"If voting ever changed anything, they'd abolish it"
Ken Livingstone

Polling stations represent one of the more devolved activities of the electoral process and, therefore, can throw up problems that are only discovered later in the process – usually at the count or, worse still, in the High Court! Thus, they are not susceptible to the normal "command-control" system of management that electoral law is based upon; the Returning Officer decides this, refuses that, allows something else, etc. Technically, decisions at polling stations are largely devolved to individual Presiding Officers to issue/refuse ballot papers, close the poll for riots, etc. which can, if not wisely made, lead to serious repercussions. Moreover, if there are some 110 polling stations (as there are in Huntingdonshire for a full election), then problems can be encountered over staffing (see Chapter 5) as well as location.

Polling station inspection

Most Returning Officers appoint staff to tour polling stations during polling day. This is a very sensible and highly recommended practice, no matter how many or how few polling stations are in the constituency/district/borough. Sometimes these "touring officers" are appointed as full powers official Deputy Returning Officers which can be useful as they can make decisions "on the spot". Sometimes, they are designated polling station Inspectors, their primary role being to check polling stations for safety, access, full complement of equipment, etc. as well as smooth operation of the process. Whatever practical arrangements are made in your area, it is worthwhile having some form of visiting/inspection regime by experienced staff who can assist a worried Presiding Officer, placate an angry elector, give out some replacement equipment or deal with an over-zealous teller.

Mobile phones are useful but there is a limit to their utility in difficult situations where an irate agent believes that his or her candidate has a genuine complaint which could lead to an election defeat.

The buildings used for polling stations vary tremendously in their quality. Many authorities still use schools (no charge for hire, but costs incurred for caretakers, heating, etc.) and the more contemporary practice is to allow the school to continue operating as normally as possible on polling day. Closing schools for this day is unpopular with both teachers and parents, particularly in early May as exams and exam preparation are in full swing at that time. On the other hand, head-teachers in particular are highly conscious of security for their pupils in today's world and having several hundred comparative "strangers" moving in and out of their premises is not an attractive option. A balance must (and can) usually be found with special access for electors, the polling station in a portakabin set apart from the main school buildings, discreet car parking, clear signage, etc. Early consultation and negotiation with the school is recommended, particularly if problems have been encountered in earlier elections.

Access issues

Access to polling stations is an issue that must be given thorough attention nowadays. Both the Electoral Commission and the Ministry of Justice take the view that the Disability Discrimination Legislation applies to the provision of facilities for voting. Returning Officers do not want to face new legal challenges in this area (running elections is complex enough!), with allegations of providing an inferior service to a person with disabilities than to a non-disabled person.

To be fair, much progress has been made in public buildings over recent years, with permanent access ramps, wide doors, low level polling booths, etc. but many venerable polling stations (often in rural areas) still do not comply with modern requirements. Moreover, in rural areas there are often no public halls in existence at all and so premises such as private houses, farm buildings, pubs, vestries in churches, etc. are pressed into service. Some of these are user-unfriendly for those who have disabilities and some Returning Officers have talked about withdrawing polling stations completely in these circumstances rather than face challenge or criticism from groups that represent the disabled. This usually produces an outcry from particular villages who have seen many of their local facilities (like the school and the post office) close over the years and now view the withdrawal of the polling station as another nail in the coffin. All these circumstances do not increase the popularity of the Returning Officer!! Temporary buildings can often provide a palliative solution if a suitable spot on the village green, pub car park, etc. can be found.

Physical accessibility is not the only issue in this context. The Electoral Administration Act (EAA) 2006 introduced a variety of new measures, including presenting electoral documentation in Braille, languages other than English and a graphical, audio format. It is thought that, for the 2007 elections, about a quarter of Returning Officers translated documents into other languages – Polish was the most popular, followed by various languages associated with the Indian sub-continent and Portuguese.

Formal provisions have now been implemented by the 2006 Act for all local authorities to have reviewed (and keep under review) their polling places by January 2008. Councils are particularly required to seek the views of people who have expertise in relation to access to premises or facilities for people who have different forms of disability.

An Electoral Commission Circular was published on this topic (EC28/2007) to give guidance and this does recognise the fair practical point that fully accessible buildings, conveniently located for electors, are not always available – indeed, there may be little choice available. However, the review must be conducted in the public domain and the authority must "seek out" the views of all interested groups – political parties, agents, disability groups, etc. A final scheme once published can be the subject of an appeal to the Electoral Commission from not less then 30 electors in the consistency or Parish Council.

Experiences at polling stations

The stories of what – allegedly – has gone on in polling stations during polling day now form part of municipal myth and legend in the world of elections. For Returning Officers, the so-called "initiative" of many Presiding Officers knows no bounds and even the most effective training fails to curb this enthusiasm. The best message to give all Presiding Officers (and more than once) is if you are stuck or encountering problems, ring the office and ask for advice. The advice might be to wait until one of the touring officers arrives and that is highly preferable to some instant decision to close the poll and move the polling station (only to be countenanced in absolute extremis).

The author can recall at an early stage in his career (as Deputy Returning Officer in a Yorkshire District) on an inspection tour, arriving at a school (with an elections officer) to find teenage pupils playing basketball in the hall, the normal location of the polling station. After some shock and puzzlement, the table with the Presiding Officer and Poll Clerk sitting behind it was located, pushed away in a corner of the hall! The author asked for an explanation of this situation and was told that the pupils were practising for the County Quarter-Finals at the weekend, the PE teacher was a determined and large gentlemen (ex-Army instructor) who thought it perfectly reasonable that electors could weave their way through the players to cast their vote and, in any event, they would finish by lunchtime. However novel, the Deputy Returning Officer did not share this view and there followed a reasonably rugged exchange of ideas with the teacher, the basketball practice concluding rapidly afterwards. There were some mild recriminations with the Deputy Returning Officer questioning the selection of that particular Presiding Officer and complaints from the school as their basketball team did not progress to the County Finals...

On another occasion, the author was telephoned at home in the evening of polling day to say that about 30 ladies in leotards were berating the Presiding Officer in a village hall as he was preventing the aerobics class from proceeding. Suggestions that the class could be held elsewhere (in the car park, it was a pleasant sunny evening) were falling on deaf ears. Eventually, the class was cancelled and normal service resumed but with a clear reminder to staff to check bookings for that hall at an early stage!

Many years ago it was frowned on if polling staff brought radios/portable TVs into the polling station to occupy the quiet hours but this is now widespread practice. If it is not interfering with issuing ballot papers, it is very hard on the staff to stop them doing this. Technically, they are not meant to leave the Station during polling hours but a measure of common sense, give and take, must prevail. Again, there are stories of staff deserting their duties for sunbathing (hot day, poor turnout on small register, boring hours to fill) or going to the pub for lunch (next door to the Station, the landlord said he would "keep an eye on things", etc.).

The author, again as a Deputy Returning Officer in North Yorkshire, recalls a by-election in February that occurred in weather entirely inconducive to sunbathing. Indeed, snow was falling heavily and the polling station was in a domestic garage with an "up and over" door. At about mid-morning, the polling staff telephoned the Council Offices saying they wanted to resign as they could not stand the cold any longer. Another difficult and frank discussion ensued with threats of criminal action (largely unspecified) and counter-threats of cruelty to staff being exchanged. Eventually, workmen (on emergency rates) were summoned from the Council's workforce and dispatched to build a temporary screen at the front of the garage. Large portable heaters were also sent out and polling facilities were restored, even though the turnout was unsurprisingly low in those weather conditions.

Another similarly awkward situation arose in the West Midlands. Reports were received that a Presiding Officer had died at a particular polling station and his body was lying on the pavement outside, surrounded by ambulance staff. An extremely callous Returning Officer asked first if polling was continuing ("Couldn't the Polling Clerk manage until we find a replacement?") but, eventually, was persuaded to visit the Station rather than reading the legislation to see if death of a Presiding Officer is covered (there is no reference to this in the Representation of the People Act). However, this story had a happy ending in that the Presiding Officer had simply had a mild fit (*petit mal*) and was not dead. He wanted to continue as a Presiding Officer later in the day but a replacement was found. Fortunately, this was a multi-use location with another polling station in the same hall so there was another experienced Presiding Officer on site to deal with the situation. The Returning Officer did raise some concerns later at the competence of the ambulance service regarding the diagnosis of death but this was vehemently disputed; the Presiding Officer went back to electoral duties at the same station in subsequent years.

At a city authority in the East, a newish Presiding Officer showed initiative (of sorts) that did cause the Returning Officer some public embarrassment. The polling station was in a school and, during the day, a team of young people serving a Community Service Order arrived to undertake gardening work. They were being sponsored by (or at least wore the uniform of) a well-known fast food chain of restaurants, featuring a colourful T-shirt. This T-shirt was the same colour as that used by a major political party for all their campaign literature, posters, etc. The young gardeners set to their tasks outside the polling station, causing no interference to the voters or, indeed, any others. However, the Presiding Officer felt that such a bold uniform could influence voters and, moreover, believed that an element of partiality was being shown to this particular party. This somewhat remarkable judgement led her to instruct the gardeners (male and female) to remove their T-shirts before continuing their work. Some refused and, highly upset, walked off the job in breach of their Order. Some remained and, in various states of *déshabille*, continued to garden. However, unsurprisingly, it was not long before the agents were notified by the tellers at the station, and the media arrived – rather routine election stories can always be spiced up with this sort of picture. More senior electoral staff arrived too late to stop the distinctly embarrassing story and photographs. The Returning Officer had much to explain away, though only after an extremely forthright private discussion with the Presiding Officer.

Tellers

Tellers can cause some problems at polling stations if they are over-zealous. New guidance was produced for the 2007 local elections with which a number of electoral practitioners were unhappy. It was produced by the Electoral Commission who said, in their defence, that their consultation on a draft did not produce much comment by way of response. The guidance confirms all the usual points about tellers having no legal status, not interfering with the smooth running of the poll, not being admitted to the polling station, etc., but does have one or two new points which did cause concern. First, they are permitted under the new guidance to approach voters on the way into the polling station, the old guidance limiting this to voters on the way out. In practice, this is understandable, as most leave their poll cards with the polling staff after voting and have no idea of their voter number on their exit; most reasonably experienced tellers knew this anyway and ignored that guidance point. This seems reasonable as long as the voter is not unduly delayed or confused by tellers as being part of the official staff. The second point is that, under the old guidance, tellers were allowed to wear rosettes (therefore, demonstrating that they were not an election official) so long as no words (party names) were included. The new guidance permits wording on the rosette but disallows T-shirts, handbags, etc. with party/candidate names. In the run-up to May 2007, a few Electoral Administrators became quite agitated and negotiated local agreements with their political parties to reflect former arrangements. Other areas reported, as usual, that the tellers (and their party organisers) had never even heard of the guidance, let alone had the opportunity of observing its content. Several Returning Officers produced a laminated copy of it for each polling station so that the Presiding Officer could show it to the various tellers to encourage their co-operation in the process. As things turned out, there were limited reports of problems in 2007, but the Commission have said they will keep the guidance under review.

With due respect to tellers, there were perhaps more important technical issues causing concern before the 2007 elections, those being more 2006 Electoral Administration Act changes. Tendered votes could now be issued to postal voters who claimed not to have so applied or so registered (depending on whether or not it was before/after 5.00pm). Initial returns showed that most areas did not issue any of these and, probably, only about one-third issued one. Similar worries were also expressed about correction of procedural errors made in connection with the register, e.g. mistaken omission of elector's name by Electoral Registration staff. This could be corrected right up to and including polling day, until 9.00pm. Again, these new powers appear to have been used very sparingly.

Security mark

For many, one of the more positive steps forward since the 2006 Act has been the ability to do away with the dreaded stamping instrument in issuing ballot papers and use a different security mark, e.g. a watermark in the paper or overprinting/underprinting. Stamping instruments (with their variable pin settings to create a perforated official mark) frequently failed by jamming or, worse still, the staff forgot to stamp an issued ballot that was then automatically disallowed at the count as not bearing the official mark. Printing something like the name of the Council with a date as an "underprint" on the ballot in the style of a bank cheque was a most successful move. The underprint could be done with ink that was not possible to photocopy – a greyish ballot paper came out with a white background that was immediately identifiable as a forgery. It was considered preferable to watermarking paper (with a civic crest, for example) as this is a slower process and if ballots (as replacements) had to be printed quickly, it might not be possible to source substantial supplies of watermarked paper quickly. Reflecting on this administrative change, it is encouraging to record at least one positive outcome from that legislation!

Chapter 3

NOMINATIONS

"I never think you should judge a country by its politics.
After all, we English are quite honest by nature, aren't we?"
Attributed to Alfred Hitchcock, spoken by Miss Froy in the
1930s film The Lady Vanishes

"He stood twice for Parliament, but so diffidently that his
candidature passed almost unnoticed"
Decline and Fall, Evelyn Waugh

The process

Nominations are one of those pivotal points of the electoral process where there is much scope for both error and pressure on Returning Officers/Electoral Administrators. The best piece of practical advice is to encourage nominations early and, if possible, by appointment. A mass of nominations coming into the office at local election time with a couple of hours to go before closure of the time period is a cocktail recipe (before the main course of polling day) that points to problems and possible disasters. It must be fairly said that most (experienced) agents are well aware of this and seek to avoid a last-minute rush but, regrettably, every year there seem to be instances where this does not happen. Some candidates appear to have an extremely casual attitude to the time limit for close of nominations. In 2007, a Returning Officer received a call from a lady who said that she had a hair appointment at a nearby town and was quite sure that the Returning Officer would be "understanding" if she brought her papers in subsequently – and well after close of nominations! Of course, the Returning Officer cannot be so flexible.

It would be encouraging to write that the rules (of which more later) introduced by the 2006 Act have improved this position, but unfortunately all they have done is simply to place another complex overlay on top of an already technical process.

Timescale

So when can the Returning Officer start accepting nomination papers to encourage early lodging? The Local Elections Rules provide that the Returning Officer must publish the Notice of Election (NoE) stating "the place and times at which the nomination papers are to be delivered". Effectively, this means that for local elections the decision rests with the Returning Officer but, for parliamentary elections, the rules (Rule 1) state that papers may be delivered between 10.00am and 4.00pm on any day after the publication of the NoE.

Such apparent differing practice within the process is a statutory feature associated with nominations – different elections have different timescales for no apparent reason! The Electoral Commission, whilst recognising this difference in practice, offer the advice that to maintain consistency the commencement period for local elections could be deferred until the day following the publication of the NoE; the utility of that is lost on the author who would much prefer a radical reform of this archaic routine.

Receipt of papers

And so to the practical receipt of papers in the office. An appointment system certainly helps – candidates and agents "dropping in" without notice at an already busy time is not helpful. Checking the papers takes time; some agents wait, others do not. Some Returning Officers/ Electoral Administrators operate an unofficial first check and, time permitting, the forms are taken away to be corrected/amended. Some do not do this and give a formal decision on the day they are received; this is in accordance with Electoral Commission advice published in March 2007, although if you received, say, 100 nominations for local elections in one day it would be simply impossible to follow. Frankly, the Electoral Commission advice may be too demanding; the official position in the rules is that you have 24 hours after close of nominations before having to publish a statement of persons nominated.

Issues with nomination papers

Nomination papers can, sometimes, be far from straightforward and it is often worthwhile taking a little time to reflect on a difficult point. Of course the Returning Officer must consider papers on their face and not become a detective to investigate behind the documentation. Moreover, the Returning Officer is making a decision on the validity of the nomination paper, not on the nomination itself. This is quite a difficult concept established in case law but if a candidate/agent produces validly completed papers that accord with the law, it is not for the Returning Officer to dispute an apparently valid address or query an age qualification (now down to 18 rather than 21).

However, problems do occur, even with these guidelines. What about the situation where apparently valid papers were received but both the Returning Officer and the agent knew (indeed the agent told the Returning Officer) that a subscriber had died since signing the form, but before the formal adjudication of its validity? This occurred in 2007 and the author agreed with a Returning Officer in the South of England that another nomination was required. The original form was not subscribed by an eligible elector and seeking another valid paper was the safest course to follow.

What about the situation where it is known to the Returning Officer that a candidate is below the age of 18? Leading Counsel supports the author's view that it is simply absurd for a Returning Officer to deny certain factual knowledge that he or she may have; the Returning Officer must point out this discrepancy to the agent/candidate (there are recently strengthened criminal penalties for false statements).

A more contentious issue developed in an authority in the Midlands in 2007 when the Returning Officer, with 40 minutes to go before nominations for the local election closed, received an email purporting to be from a local political office "countermanding" the right of an individual to use an already authorised party description; apparently the individual concerned had had a serious fallout with a regional officer of the party, hence the email. To make matters worse, the Returning Officer was dealing with that nomination when the email arrived. What to do?

The view taken was to proceed with the nomination, the candidate having appeared with perfectly valid paperwork including authorisation to use the party name. The email claimed to be from an individual in the regional party headquarters, but the entirely proper view was taken that the email could not withdraw/countermand valid papers. The dispute was between the party and the individual candidate (no sign of the agent) and the Returning Officer should not be drawn into that, seeking only to process valid, on their face, papers.

Minor errors

Powers introduced in 2007 allow Returning Officers to correct minor errors made on nomination papers; the rules give a couple of examples, namely errors as to an electoral number or obvious spelling mistakes. Great care is needed here and it is suggested that this power is exercised in a very constructive and careful way. Thus, an absence of an electoral number on the form would *not*, in the author's view, be a minor error and, therefore, should not be corrected by the Returning Officer/Electoral Administrator. A simple transposition of a couple of digits (otherwise correct) in the number would probably constitute a minor error.

Omission of a party name is not a minor error. At an authority in 2007, the Returning Officer received papers via the post for a valid nomination in favour of a particular party but the description was omitted from the actual nomination paper. Attached to the papers were valid authorisation papers from the party; the Returning Officer telephoned the candidate inviting him to repair the omission but was dismissed in a perfunctory way with "you can do what you like" or similar less gracious words. The Returning Officer allowed the nomination to go forward but the candidate had no description.

Another more amusing incident occurred at the same authority where a parish council candidate (of no party affiliation) completed the description with "6ft tall, blue eyes, greying hair". The Returning Officer asked the candidate if he really wanted this on the ballot paper and would he not prefer "independent", albeit that this may not be so personalised or distinctive. Again, the candidate was very dismissive, but the nomination contained (perhaps unsurprisingly) several other serious errors and was disallowed.

There are now powers to accept commonly used names of candidates as opposed to their actual names. The Returning Officer has a discretion here and must be satisfied that any commonly used names are not likely to mislead or confuse electors and are not obscene or offensive. This appears not to have caused too many problems in 2007 and most authorities usually have at least one candidate in the local elections using a commonly used first name. Use of a commonly used surname is more spasmodic.

Party names

In 2007 some problems arose regarding local party names. The statutory position is that parties can register up to 12 names with the Electoral Commission and no other descriptions are permitted. Some smaller regional or local parties registered very specific names, such as:

- "Faversham First!"

- "Sittingbourne First!"

- "Palaid Cymm – Save Withybush Hospital"

- "People's Voice Torfaen".

This provoked controversy amongst opposing candidates and the national parties who said they were disadvantaged at local level because their descriptions were more national based and, therefore, generalised. However, despite the pressure put on certain Returning Officers, they had no discretion to refuse properly registered names. Furthermore, the Electoral Commission point out that, similarly, they have no discretion and *must* register names that meet the relevant statutory criteria. However, it is understood that the Commission will be having consultation with the political parties to consider this issue further.

Deposit money

Finally, a nomination is not complete without receipt of the deposit money. A remarkable variety of amounts are now required for different types of election (e.g. £500 for a Westminster parliamentary election) but the traditional approach was that it should be received in cash or by banker's draft; cheques can be stopped or bounce. The Electoral Administration Act 2006 has introduced changes in that, with the Returning Officer's consent, debit/credit cards and electronic transfer of funds may be employed. Some guidance from either the Ministry of Justice or Electoral Commission will be received on this before the next general election and many Returning Officers are not particularly attracted by the prospect of registering as individual merchants to handle credit card transactions. Whilst the electoral world must move on, some further clarification is needed here.

(For a more detailed consideration of the nomination process, Shaw's have a separate booklet on this topic written by the current author.)

Chapter 4

THE COUNT

"Let him that hath understanding count the number..."
Revelations 13(18)

"He stood and counted them...and cursed his luck"
A E Housman

Electoral Commission guidance issued in 2007 describes the count "as usually the most pressurised and potentially difficult part of the electoral process...stress levels can be high...but can be very exciting". It would be easy – and perhaps a little churlish – to take an entirely different view. Processing nominations can be highly stressful. Even dealing with postal votes and awkward applications for registration with a time limit ticking against the Returning Officer/Electoral Administrator have more than a frisson of tension. Moreover, many counts can be entirely routine and almost prosaic, especially when the result is never in doubt. Regrettably, it is the author's experience that, at many Town and Parish Council counts, candidates do not even bother to attend.

Planning and preparation

Nevertheless, there must always be considerable effort applied to planning and executing any count if a successful outcome is to be achieved – no matter how many times Councillor X has won this seat on the District Council (one of the author's members has held a particular ward for approaching 50 years!).

To key issues then at the outset. Should alcohol be served at the count? Many public halls/sports halls have bars that stay open during the count (within licensing hours) and sell alcohol to agents, candidates and their supporters (certainly not the staff!). At the last Euro Election (2005), in the Eastern Region a number of the candidates (plus their entourages) spent the majority of the Sunday afternoon/evening in a sports hall bar watching an international soccer match. Indeed, some expressed great anger and outrage when the bar closed at 11.00pm that Sunday evening, nearly an hour before the result was announced! Other venues have no such facilities and, indeed, do not have a public gallery. Admission to these counts for the public is a matter for the Returning Officer, but it is not automatic to subscribe to the Electoral Commission view that "it is a good idea to ban alcohol at the count until after the announcement of the results"; local decisions and circumstances should prevail.

Smoking is no longer allowed in view of the 2007 legislation and the use of mobile phones (and similar) should be confined to an area outside the counting room.

Selection of the count venue and the starting time of the count are clearly of paramount importance. Some Returning Officers still choose very small rooms because the sports hall is in use for a fitness class or the school might need the hall if the barbecue is rained off, etc., etc. Surely democracy at either local or national level is worthy of greater consideration and, indeed, precedence? Or possibly not? – a very recent problem arose in the East when a ballroom dancing class had to terminate (at a hall in a FE college) to allow count tables, chairs and equipment to be set up. The precedence of local democracy was vigorously disputed by the dancers and, much to the chagrin of the Returning Officer, only received tepid, forced support from the college authorities. Never presume that because you have always held the count in that hall on the first Thursday evening in May since time immemorial that such arrangements continue in perpetuity – it is always best to check and rebook a couple of months beforehand and remember that you do need the hall several hours before close of poll to set up properly.

Thursday evening or Friday morning?

Timing of the count became something of an issue in 2007 with the later 10.00pm close of poll and the practical applications of undertaking personal identifier verification of those postal votes returned to polling stations during the day. A sensible step at any count now is to have a special team of "better" counters at a table ready to deal with postal votes brought in to polling stations during the day. Counts have been known to be delayed because of this factor not being catered for. For 2007 the Electoral Commission reported that this was not too significant a problem because, by then, staff were used to the verification process. In addition, a good number of Returning Officers had arranged for postal votes to be collected in during the day and processed, reducing the numbers to be opened on the night.

The actual test for the Returning Officer – to start the count as soon as practicable after the close of poll – was further complicated by considerable political/media pressure. Expectations for a Thursday night count in certain areas are very strong and not easily resisted. In 2007, 50% of counts (numbering approximately 150) were held over until Friday morning, though Scotland and Wales started on Thursday night. Declarations of results came in the early hours of the morning through to breakfast time.

Recruiting any election staff nowadays is generally not easy (see Chapter 5) and many people do not view the prospect of sitting up through the night at a local sports hall for very modest remuneration as at all attractive. The "usual suspects" of earlier years, bank and building society staff, are not really interested and the advent of ATMs means that old-fashioned skills of counting bank-notes quickly are dying out. Most count staff are found from the ranks of local authority employees (past and present), as well as those with some connection with this sector (parish clerks, etc.), together with their friends and family.

Not all Returning Officers agree with the Electoral Commission advice that, if counting immediately following close of poll, it is preferable not to use staff that have been out all day on polling duty. Presiding Officers will have to bring their boxes (and other paperwork) into a count venue and most (although not all) think that, once there, they may as well stay for the count. Some authorities have insisted that Presiding Officers remain at the count in case there are queries over a ballot paper account, tendered vote, etc.

However, the experience of the 2007 local elections confirms the view that overnight counts are increasingly difficult to staff; for those counts, polling station staff and others, who had already completed a full day's work had to step in. Exhaustion of all concerned is a potential risk factor in respect of both the efficient conduct of the count and, more significantly, the accuracy of the results. For the Assembly elections in Wales (2007), there was a venue in the south of the Principality where there were four recounts and the Returning Officer was eventually obliged to send staff home and bring in fresh teams. Some regional results were not declared until the Friday afternoon. The experience of those who started counting on the Friday was overwhelmingly more positive. Most counts proceeded well following a start around 9.00am and were completed by early or mid-afternoon that same day.

The Thursday night/Friday morning issue will undoubtedly be revisited in future years. Friday morning counts are not unusual where combined polls have been held (local/parliamentary quite common now) and, to avoid some of the risks referred to, they should seriously be considered as the most effective practical option.

Staffing

There is a requirement for several key staff at a count who are, perhaps, even more needed than the Returning Officer! The Chief Executive of a London Borough once said that the function of the Returning Officer at the count was simply to "look decorous"!

The Count

A reception table at the count entrance operated by two or three officers who know the process is highly desirable. Unfortunately, there is sometimes a newish Presiding Officer who has felt unwell, endured abuse and a power cut at his/her station, then arrives at the count venue late (car breakdown) utterly confused, not even knowing what a ballot paper account is, let alone having completed it. These harassed individuals usually have the election paperwork scattered on the back seat of their car with the dead battery of their mobile phone. The best plan is that they are taken to a quiet corner and "assisted" to complete the paperwork in some sort of reasonable order. However well the count is planned, it only takes one box or a missing ballot paper account to cause serious problems downstream; early action to prevent this is essential.

A PR/media person(s) to deal with the press/tv/radio is also essential. This is particularly true if you have a high profile count or, worse still, appear to be in trouble! (Winchester, General Election 1977 is a good example of this and is quoted extensively at Chapter 7 dealing with the media.)

Team leaders/count supervisors have to be experienced in the process and able to push tiring counters along. At some counts they need to be reasonably robust too if constantly harangued by over-eager candidates and agents. They also need to be shrewd enough not to make naïve statements in front of the scrutineers: "...this Presiding Officer always has tendered papers in his box...we'll never get this box verified even if we count it 50 times...don't take too long, any figure within 20 or 30 will do..." These and many other entirely unhelpful comments have fallen from the lips of staff who, although they should know better, say regrettable and embarrassing things when tired and fed up with the process.

Police presence at counts is very variable these days. Clearly, with high profile counts they will carry out searches beforehand but, at local elections, they will probably only visit briefly during the evening/ morning. Local liaison is important and having out-of-hours contact numbers essential.

Emergency planning

Bomb threats and fire scares are not unknown at counts. The key point is to have some sort of contingency plan to relocate the count to another venue, probably the next day. The safety of people is the utmost priority and their speedy evacuation (without ballot boxes) is more important than counting ballots – always remember elections can be re-run.

Doubtful ballot papers

There is considerable guidance already published by both Shaws and the Electoral Commission on dealing with doubtful ballot papers. For Returning Officers and Deputy Returning Officers, it is worthwhile having a very clear "slot" allocated to deal with these papers, not leaving it until the very end of the count. Agents are entitled to challenge decisions but it is important to remember that it is the Returning Officer making the final decision, however unpopular that verdict may be. Some Returning Officers try to speed up this process by giving generic instructions to automatically allow ticks in place of crosses and throw out all blanks. As long as you have some experienced team leaders who can implement these steps and the Returning Officer feels confident with their approach then that is fine, but always be mindful of the old adage that counts should be accurate and acceptable rather than fast.

Counting methods

Similar considerations apply to different counting methods, particularly for multi-member wards; grass skirts, counting sheets, etc. are all in common usage with some local adaptations. Again, this is a matter for local decision making. Often, more time is spent physically sorting the papers into separate piles than actually counting. The European election ballot paper is always large and many voters feel the need to fold into it the smaller local paper, often with some intricate origami! At the 2004 elections this took many hours to separate, the staff having to stand over their tables simply separating the ballots. As yet, it is believed that no machine is being developed (or even invented) to do this, apart from a human being!

Draft result and recounts

It is the practice of virtually all Returning Officers to show candidates and their agents a draft result. If it is close, it is best practice for the Returning Officer to ask for a least one recount and just advise candidates/agents what is happening; if they are following the count, they will not be surprised and will hopefully be impressed by the care being taken to deliver an accurate result. They can ask for recounts, but Returning Officers have to take a sensible view and decline spurious requests or pleas to save a deposit. Many new Returning Officers ask how close the result should be for a recount to be required and how many times is it reasonable to recount. The answer is that there can be no absolute golden rule. A single figure majority of victory would probably warrant more than one recount and it is always worrying when further recounts produce totally different results. A method sometimes used in those circumstances is to break the count down into parts and get agents to "sign off" papers in smaller numbers (perhaps in different parts of the hall), thereby achieving agreed figures to contribute to the overall total. It is slow, time-consuming, tiring work when everyone is very tired already...but it is probably better than facing an election petition...

"Tidying up"

On a more mundane point, it is worthwhile "tidying up" and sorting out all the associated packages from the polling stations as the count proceeds. Having a small team behind the scenes to sort out all the papers that appear at the count is much to be preferred to having to start on this task after the last result is declared. For those who have not seen behind the scenes at a count before, it is amazing as to the amount of material to be sorted before storage. It is worthwhile trying to get it into some sort of order too – there is nothing worse than ending up in front of a High Court Judge or Master waiting for a particular envelope to be opened and hoping that it does actually contain what it should! Again, it has been known for the police to obtain court orders in criminal proceedings to examine certain ballot papers. If they are all thrown in heaps at the back of a municipal depot they (and, possibly, the delayed court) are not going to be too pleased to wait while your staff sort through a mountain of sacks. Also, it is important to have a process that gets empty ballot boxes out of the hall when empty **only** – boxes should not be left with uncounted papers but, unfortunately, this has occurred in some places.

Most counts run smoothly but the main political parties complain that count practices vary widely. There are usually complaints about slowness and poor communication at counts – candidates and agents are not sure what stage the count has reached. Whilst there may be some truth in these complaints, it is reasonable to expect candidates/ agents to concentrate and keep up with the progress of the count; many of them know the process as well as the staff. However, it is always good practice for Returning Officers to announce that, for instance, verification is complete, counting is about to begin, please come forward to see a draft result, etc. On the whole, most candidates and agents are satisfied with the count and thank the Returning Officer and staff for all their hard work.

Chapter 5

APPOINTING STAFF

In this chapter we shall consider both the permanent and temporary staff that Returning Officers (not local authorities) employ during election periods. Clearly, the competence and quality of both groups of staff can mean the difference between an efficiently run election and appearances in the courts facing petitions and other proceedings. So this is very important!

Permanent staff

Most local authorities employ full-time permanent election staff who undertake registration duties as well as organising elections. Some smaller District Councils try to combine these roles with other administrative tasks in an effort to be economical but this is getting more difficult as pressures in this area of work grow; in 2007, the Electoral Commission published draft performance indicators for registration work. To achieve these will require greater effort in a number of Councils.

The actual number employed varies considerably from authority to authority: two or three is quite typical in the Districts while large metropolitan authorities would have many more – 12 to 20 perhaps. Whatever this dedicated number is, there is the great tradition of augmenting the basic team with additions at election time. Some of these are part-timers, often brought in from outside the authority to undertake a wide variety of mainly clerical tasks. Others are much more senior, often, though not always, from the Council's own legal and administrative sections and are people with considerable practical experience of running counts, polling stations, etc. Some of these may be appointed as Deputy Returning Officers, some polling station inspectors to tour on polling day, some team leaders at the count, etc. The real point of all this is that the traditional method of deploying staff to run elections is in this way – it is considered to be efficient in that already employed staff are used to tackle a peak of work. However, it is now emerging that this traditional method is under threat. The following is a quote from a District Council Chief Executive (Returning Officer) in the East Midlands, speaking in June 2007:

> *"My election staff are both on the point of retirement and they are both now desperate to go. This election was by far the worst, most complicated and stressful experience they have had in 20-odd years – and we didn't have the software problems and only half our wards were contested. If they feel that way I am sure others feel similar or worse. I worry where we're going to get elections staff from in the future if the system isn't radically simplified."*

Other Councils were reporting similar problems after past elections. Over the last few years, it has become more and more difficult to recruit staff for these permanent posts. The well-publicised problems in the process in recent years have simply compounded the difficulties and lessened the attractiveness of these jobs. Despite the AEA (and others) running both qualification and training courses, the supply of suitable candidates to meet demand is not sufficient. Eventually, this will impact on the staff management model outlined above and the only short-term solution will surely involve taking more time from the permanent staff that augment the central team around mid-April until early May. Several authorities have been forced into doing this already with solicitors, chartered secretaries, etc. spending much more of their time on the actual detailed organisation of the poll. Other authorities have recruited recently retired staff as a short-term solution (often via the AEA Consultancy Service) and others have "borrowed" people from Councils without elections for a particular year (remember authorities have different electoral cycles, both on an area and time basis). However, none of these approaches are substantive long-term solutions. Are there any other more viable solutions to the problem?

"Shared services"

On the basis that suitable recruits are unlikely to be forthcoming (but efforts must still be made in that direction), another approach is "shared services". One of the new concepts in local government, the idea of councils combining to deliver services, is becoming ever more popular. It is seen as a way to both reduce costs and be resilient in meeting staff shortages. Its applicability – and popularity – is seen as being strongest with back office functions of a largely administrative nature. There would certainly be some scope in the field of elections for both formal and informal co-operation between authorities. There is a measure of informal co-operation now in sharing of advice, training, equipment, etc. but the scope is there for development. More formal arrangements could be made between Returning Officers to organise particular functions – for example, where, at a parliamentary election the constituency crosses a local authority boundary, and local elections are being held at the same time, then one Returning Officer would usually appoint polling station staff who would automatically also administer the parliamentary responsibilities at those stations, albeit not within a constituency for which that Returning Officer was responsible. This could be extended, possibly, to other parts of the process such as dealing with nominations. It is accepted that this might be controversial in that agents/candidates may not wish to travel to another office for this purpose, but it has already been seriously considered. At the 2005 General Election, one Acting Returning Officer was considering appointing the Chief Executive of a neighbouring authority as Deputy Acting Returning Officer for her constituency as it straddled two local authority boundaries. Eventually, local circumstances arose that precluded this, but those involved at the time thought the idea entirely workable, if not entirely popular with candidates and agents from that constituency. Another example is printing. For the 2007 Sedgefield parliamentary by-election, postal vote stationery was provided to the Acting Returning Officer at Sedgefield Council by Sunderland City Print, Sunderland City Council's in-house printing unit.

In reality, more study and research work is needed to develop models of good practice of joint working on elections. Unfortunately, a bid to secure funds for such work was refused by the Regional Centre of Excellence (Eastern) in 2007 – these organisations fund studies in other areas such as procurement and financial management. The bid (made by the author) is currently being discussed very informally with officials at the Electoral Policy Division at the Ministry of Justice.

Temporary staff

"Well-trained and helpful staff are the most important resource at a polling station."

This statement from an Electoral Commission training manual is entirely correct but, for many involved in the elections world, something of a counsel of perfection. The days of Electoral Administrators having lists of willing, experienced and highly competent staff to choose from are long gone. Today, all authorities report difficulties in recruiting staff for all aspects of election work, whether at polling stations, the counting hall or assisting with the dispatch of postal votes. For local authority staff it is no longer perceived as a plum job with attractive pay rates. The majority of Returning Officers probably employ a greater proportion of staff from outside their authorities; those from contracted-out services, recently retired, parish clerks, friends and relatives of staff, etc. Most of those undertaking these duties do so mainly out of sense of civic and national duty and the habitual "we have always done this on the first Thursday in May". Their ages rather betray their provenance from a deference culture that has long since faded to insignificance in our civil society. Of course, some (comparatively) younger staff from local government ranks do work on elections, but it is getting more and more difficult every year to retain their services and encourage others. Most of these staff have difficult and demanding day jobs at the Town Hall and to lose a couple of days (training, poll and count) simply means tougher work in the following week. Sitting in a draughty church hall for some 15 hours for £100–£150 net has pretty pallid attractions when, if you are taking time away from the office, a day's relaxation at the coast or in the countryside is also on offer – admittedly unpaid, but there are a significant number of staff at middle levels in local government who complain of not being able to take their full holiday entitlements (and are reminded so by their families...).

So, can further steps be taken to improve the situation? Is more money the answer? All fees could be usefully increased (discussed later in Chapter 13) and, as a chief officer once pointed out to the author, "cash is always handy...". More training and support to staff would be another step forward; the 1999 European parliamentary election saw the first really large training exercise. Most authorities now have some sort of training prior to every election and 2007 was no exception with all the new provisions of the Electoral Administration Act 2006 (plus supporting secondary legislation) to absorb and impart to staff. However, time and money has to be found for all this amongst the already busy and crowded working life of local government; it can be done but it is demanding. Remember, on polling day most Returning Officers employ hundreds of staff.

The most significant change would be to increase interest in the process of "delivering democracy" – a fundamental part of our tolerant and liberal society. However, declining turnouts on polling day are indicative of the diminishing interest in politics (and politicians) in our country. Cynicism, particularly amongst the young, is not excluded from the ranks of the public sector and it is fascinating to note that Returning Officers have been given new duties to increase turnout amongst the electorate (Electoral Administration Act 2006). However, many Returning Officers/Electoral Administrators believe we should start nearer to home with our staff, encouraging them to become involved. Little thought is given to this theme either at the Electoral Commission or in Whitehall for the simple reason that every year

Returning Officers just manage to get by and deliver results that are only rarely challenged and, if so challenged, only in very few places. The resourcefulness of staff in local government is well known, but in the electoral field virtually legendary. Can it continue or, more pointedly, is it a good idea to keep putting this resourcefulness to the test?

Age and experience

Reference has already been made to the advanced age of a considerable number of, particularly, Presiding Officers. This is significant in the insurance context for many policies exclude those of a certain age – usually 65/70. Liability for the employment of staff still rests with the Returning Officer, so it is worthwhile checking this point. Some companies will extend cover for a day or so when circumstances are explained and it is simply vital not to lose the services of experienced Presiding Officers in their late 60s and early 70s. The worst scenario is for claims to arise from these people against the Returning Officer (as employer), only to find the insurance companies vitiating their policies. This is trouble all round…

Most Returning Officers/Electroral Administrators follow the practice of only appointing a Presiding Officer once they have successfully carried out the duties of a Poll Clerk a couple of times. This is entirely sensible as it builds up both experience and confidence in recent new recruits that cannot be supplied by any amount of training. Obviously, with the pressures of staff recruitment already discussed, this does not get easier, but it is still a worthwhile guideline. Some are too nervous or lacking in self-confidence to take the step up, but this can often be addressed by putting them in a dual station alongside a more experienced Presiding Officer. Again, it is worthwhile leaving the more robust and experienced Presiding Officers in the busier (usually more urban) stations, for it is in these that voter peaks often occur in the early evening after people have finished work for the day, watched Coronation Street on television and are taking the dog for a walk after supper/dinner/tea (depending on which part of the country you live in) on the way to the pub for a drink, etc! Where there are 20 people in the queue waiting to vote and they are being delayed by someone who "always votes here" but whose name is not on the register ("but we always fill the form in and send it back every year"), you need a Presiding Officer of sufficient composure and experience to deal with the situation. If the name is not on the register, they are *not* going to vote, despite their references to previous years. They should be referred to a helpline, hopefully provided to the election office as the Returning Officer now has powers to remedy certain situations of this type.

Long hours – at the count or not?

Staff clearly work long hours on polling duties and even longer hours if engaged in a count on the evening of polling day. A number of staff (and Returning Officers) have queried this in recent years in the context of the European Working Time and Young Workers Directives (The Working Time Regulations of 1998). The admirable aim of these rules is to prevent employees working excessive hours but there can be exceptions in certain circumstances; electoral work is just such a case in point. The Returning Officer, as employer, needs to organise this with his/her staff so that rights under the Directive are modified or, better still, set aside. It is usual practice to include a waiver in the appointment letter to individual staff.

The issue of long hours raises the question of whether or not Presiding Officers/Poll Clerks should be (automatically?) recruited for the count or not. Practice varies considerably here. Some Returning Officers take the view that polling staff are tired after their work during the day and should not continue into the count. However, as it is becoming more popular to count on Friday morning nowadays, this view is less convincing. Others take the view that it is essential to have Presiding Officers at the count in case any queries arise over the accuracy of their ballot paper account – but they may have a "reception committee" waiting for the Presiding Officers when they arrive at the counting hall to clarify any of these issues. Other Returning Officers are just happy to get anyone to count, whether or not they have been on duty during the day! It is probably not a good idea to have count team leaders as Presiding Officers during the day for they are key personnel and, if they are delayed in arriving for the count, arrangements can be disrupted.

On a totally morbid note, the author is sometimes asked if Presiding Officers die at their polling stations and, more urgently, if they do what happens next? Death is no respecter of persons or situations and, unfortunately, although rare, this does occur. The official advice is that the poll must continue and another Presiding Officer must be appointed at once. This is often harder to achieve in practice but Poll Clerks can generally be guided by telephone in the short term and, if touring officers/station inspectors are nearby, some temporary arrangements can be made. Returning Officers can be accused of being cold and callous in such cases but this role attracts a variety of often unpleasant soubriquets.

Recent problems at a Northern authority

It is interesting to close this chapter with an actual report on staffing from a reasonably large district council (population 130,000 plus) in North West England following the May 2007 local elections:

"Identifying sufficient staff to run elections is becoming more difficult especially with the increase in postal votes. There are currently over 250 people required for an election – this covers polling station staff, postal vote openings, poll card deliverers and count staff. Whilst some external staff are employed, a large number come from within the Council and with increasing pressures on services Service Heads are finding it more difficult to release staff to assist with election duties during office hours.

Appointing Staff

Staffing the 122 polling stations proved extremely challenging this year. It is difficult to attract people to work on polling stations for 15+ hours and it is clear that adequate monetary reward is a factor in attracting staff. There has been a move for local authorities to pay the level of pay set for parliamentary elections in order to attract enough staff, particularly now that the hours of poll have been aligned. This year the Council increased the level of pay for Presiding Officers and Poll Clerks substantially from the previous elections four years ago but it was still £30 below the parliamentary rate set in 2005 and it will be necessary to consider a further substantial rise in budgeting for the next Council elections. The County Council were faced with a similar dilemma in respect of their budgeting in 2005 and responded with a significant increase to enable fees to match the rates being paid for parliamentary election work. This means that during the 4/5 year cycle of elections pay for working on the district elections is now noticeably lower than for any other elections.

The Review of Polling Districts and Places required by the Electoral Administration Act 2006 will commence shortly, and the Returning Officer is also taking the opportunity to review the provision of polling stations at the same time. All councillors will have an opportunity to comment on their ward. With the increase in postal voters comes a decrease in electors using polling stations even where turnout levels are maintained or there has been a small rise and it may be that reducing the number of polling stations, particularly where there are currently double stations in one building could assist by reducing the number of staff required on Election day."

The review referred to above is really to tackle access issues for those with mobility problems and is certainly not designed to deal with staff recruitment problems, though it is noteworthy to see the provisions utilised in this way.

Chapter 6

CANDIDATES AND AGENTS

Relationships with the Returning Officer

For those charged with administering elections, dealing with candidates and agents can highlight both the best and worst aspects of human behaviour. Clearly, it is important to have clear lines of communication at particular times during the electoral process but, especially for the inexperienced Returning Officer, pitching the relationship at the right level is often difficult and occasionally highly challenging. Thus for local elections many of the candidates will be known personally to the Returning Officer as (probably) Chief Executive of the Council; he will be working virtually daily with the leading members as part of an executive. Indeed, at any successful local authority there will be a close link between the Chief Executive and Leader (or Group Leaders in some hung councils) if the council is to have any chance of serving its local populace well.

However, this close relationship cannot spill over into the electoral process during the run-up to the May elections (or even a by-election). Here the Chief Executive is now acting as an independent Returning Officer not susceptible to political control and direction. There must be no hint of any bias to favour the Leader or controlling group, or actions that could be construed as negative to the opposition. To be fair, many experienced local members both understand and appreciate this point but, unfortunately, there are some who still seek to push at the boundaries of this envelope. It has been known, for instance, in the case of calling a by-election, for a Returning Officer to be pressed to fix the date either earlier or later to "catch out" the other side who may not have selected a candidate quickly enough or whose candidate has to make a business trip to the USA for two weeks and so will not be able to canvass personally. It should be left to the Returning Officer to fix the date of a by-election (within the appropriate window after requisition), although it has been known for some County Returning Officers to canvass their group leaders/group whips for suitable dates (remember, Counties generally ask Districts to run their elections). In this case, the Deputy Returning Officer at District level is "instructed" to hold the election on a certain date. The formality of that instruction must be questionable. Suppose the Deputy Returning Officer chooses another date? It is submitted that there could be no formal challenge, but presumably much political acrimony and threats of reprisals. Remember too that in many parts of the two-tier system, an increasing number of members are "twin trackers" in that they serve a District/Borough as well as County, increasing the opportunity for political pressure to be put on the Deputy Returning Officer at District level.

Some authorities have unwritten protocols that their chief officers will not appear at public meetings with their members after notice of election has been published – usually around 25th March for the first Thursday in May elections. This can cause problems, for the work of local authorities does not stop if a third of the council is seeking re-election – problems occur in a whole variety of fields that often involve public consultation meetings and there is some member expectation of high-level support at these events. The profile of these issues usually grows in the run-up to an election and for a leading member to be told that he/she will not enjoy publicly exhibited support a week or two before polling day often generates a pretty volatile reaction. Controversial proposals like hospital closures, airport extensions, new roads, etc. grab the headlines and public attention. Central government have sometimes postponed consultation on the line of a new road during an election period (the A14 in Cambridge was a good example in 2006/07), but the Cambridgeshire Primary Care Trust (PCT) proceeded with the consultation process over the future of a local district hospital right through the election period. Some careful manoeuvring was required here as the Chief Executive of the relevant District Council (the author) was asked as an independent person to chair various public consultation meetings organised by the PCT; meetings selected were outside the geographical area and/or electoral timetable.

Candidates and candidature

The title "candidate" is significant for it entitles that person to be treated in a certain way – for instance, receiving copies of the register, nomination packs, using rooms for meetings, etc. Candidates at a local government election are entitled, on request to the Electoral Registration Officer, to a free copy of the *full* electoral register for the ward they are contesting. These are usually now supplied in data form, unless a paper copy is requested. The significance of these apparently helpful and straightforward rules should not be underestimated. It has been known for a prospective (undeclared) candidate to show an interest in a particular ward and be given, quite gratuitously, a sample extract from the appropriate register as an aide (before the notice of election was published), for some people have never seen an electoral register before. Those exact circumstances occurred recently in the East of England and there was clearly a misunderstanding for the lady concerned then went on to stand as an independent candidate in the local elections and did *not* request a full copy of that ward register. It was discovered later that she laboured under the misapprehension that her sample extract was the full and up-to-date register. Hence, she did not canvass a considerable number of houses. She lost at the poll, but not by a massive margin, and was invited by one of her successful opponents to a celebration barbecue the following weekend. It was only at this social event that she discovered the ward was much bigger than she originally thought. By the following week, angry letters were being received at the council offices claiming that she had been seriously misled and threatening legal action; the Returning Officer (not unknown to the author) had to advise her on petitions to challenge election results. The unsuccessful candidate's background was in market research and she claimed that, extrapolating figures in a way only she could understand indicated that, had she canvassed the (to her) unknown properties, she would have been successfully elected – top of the poll, indeed, according to her detailed calculations. There followed a number of reasonably acrimonious meetings between the lady in question and several council election staff at which various unpleasant threats were made, but the Returning Officer took no further action and no election petition materialised. Eventually, all the problems went away but the lady in question stood for election again the following year, although on this occasion for a mainstream political party; she is now both a county and town councillor.

So when does candidature begin? This used to be important in the context of electoral expenses which have to be declared at the end of the electoral process. Under the current rules, however, expenses can count as election expenses irrespective of the time when they were incurred and whether or not the candidate in question was successful. Returning Officers/Electoral Administrators should be very cautious and highly reluctant about giving "official" advice on these points, however helpful one wishes to be to "customers". This is a very technical and complex area best left to candidates, agents and their central offices.

Nevertheless, as we have seen above, candidates do have certain rights and responsibilities so it is worthwhile knowing when these arise. Broadly speaking, in the case of a General Election, a person becomes a candidate on the date of the dissolution of Parliament or, for by-elections, on the date of the occurrence of the vacancy, *if* on or before that date he/she is declared (personally or by others) to be a candidate. Later declarations can take place, if the foregoing does not apply, up to the end of the nomination period. For European elections, the regulations state that a candidate is a person who is either included in the list from a registered party or is nominated as an individual candidate.

For local elections, the guidance from the Electoral Commission for 2007 is helpful:

"...a person will become a candidate either:

- *on the last day for publication of the Notice of Election,* **Tuesday 27 March 2006** *if they or others have declared to be a candidate on or before that date, or*

- *otherwise, after* **Tuesday 27 March 2006**, *on the date on which they declare, or are declared by others, to be a candidate or are nominated as a candidate at that election, whichever is the earlier.*

Some examples of how this worked in practice:

- *A person is declared by their local political party to be a candidate for election in* **February 2007**. *They become a candidate on the last day for publication of the Notice of Election,* **Tuesday 27 March 2006**.

- *A person declares themselves to be a candidate for election on* **Wednesday 29 March 2007**. *They become a candidate on* **Wednesday 29 March 2006**.

- *A person has not been declared by themselves or another to be a candidate for election, but delivers valid nomination papers to the Returning Officer on* **Wednesday 4 April 2006**. *They become a candidate on* **Wednesday 4 April 2006**."

Appointment of agents

Candidates are not obliged to appoint agents but in practice virtually all do so, although some independent candidates do not and therefore act as their own agent which is the rule in the case of non-appointment. A candidate at a Parish Council election in England or a Community Council election in Wales need not have an election agent. The law is drafted in this negative permissive way so, presumably, it would be possible to have an agent. Thus, it has been known in Districts and Boroughs where there are joint elections with Parishes for an agent to act in both capacities. Recently, a Parish Council candidate in the Home Counties wished to appoint an agent using the common law power to do so; the Returning Officer at that authority consulted the author but both professed equal ignorance as to the source of this power!

The election timetable will have a cut-off date for notification of the agent to the Returning Officer: in the 2007 local elections it was noon on Wednesday 11th April. There is no prescribed document for this purpose and some Returning Officers produce (or obtain from companies like Shaw's) a standard form to help. There are complex rules as to the agent's office address so that, for instance, it must be within the same local government area that the election is being held, within the parliamentary constituency or constituencies which the local authority area contains, etc. (special rules apply for Wales and London too).

Once agents have been appointed, all dealings with the Returning Officer and his staff should be through them and *not* the candidates. In the 21st Century, there are not many full-time professional agents left and agents are often just appointed for particular elections. For local elections, this will often be an existing elected member or, for parliamentary elections, a secondee from a trade union. The Electoral Commission guidance rather unflatteringly states that "there are no particular qualifications for an election agent" but, certainly, the larger parties try to organise some form of training and produce notes to update their agents on the latest legislation. One advantage of being a Returning Officer (or partner of the same) is that you are specifically forbidden to be an agent!

It must be fairly recorded that Returning Officers have varying qualities of experience in dealing with agents. Most try to organise an informal meeting with them shortly after the close of nominations to advise on postal vote opening, procedure at the count, security, arrangements for the media, etc. These meetings are usually reasonably well received, although it has been known for some independent candidates to perceive them as biased in favour of the mainstream parties. Thus, at one meeting, a Returning Officer (in the chair) was asked if he could explain the role and functions of an agent to someone carrying out those duties for the first time. The Returning Officer was not given a chance to answer as other experienced agents shouted this request down, explaining very firmly that this was not the role of the Returning Officer and certainly not the function of this meeting. Cordial relationships were also strained considerably at a European Parliamentary agents' meeting in 2004 when a particular candidate (acting as his own agent) accused the Returning Officer of being a mere puppet of Brussels (he did not care for the detailed elections rules) and insisted on making his own minutes of the meeting. This gentleman's behaviour continued to deteriorate and the Returning Officer indicated he would call the police to have him ejected; fortunately, the angry candidate left, shouting threats and expletives. Such occurrences are rare and most agents are grateful for contact with the Returning Officer and receipt of information at the earliest possible stage. Strangely, there is a sense of camaraderie and gallows humour amongst the more experienced agents who inevitably complain to each other about the shortcomings of their own candidates; this is a very strange British quirk!

Behaviour of agents and candidates

Different stages of the electoral process sometimes produce unorthodox behaviour from candidates and their agents. Many have clearly led a life "untrammelled by normality" (a description applied to a moderately high profile current MP) and pay scant regard to either the formal law or well-established conventions surrounding elections. Thus, at a recent parliamentary election, a high profile media celebrity sought to commandeer a room in the council offices to give a speech (plus press conference) immediately following the deposit of his nomination papers to stand as an independent candidate. The Returning Officer pointed out that this was not possible (the room was needed for another meeting) and, in any event, such partiality could not be shown to any one candidate, no matter how high his profile in the media. As ever, the Returning Officer was accused of petty-minded bureaucracy, being negative to this candidate so as to favour the larger mainstream parties, etc. Despite these and other more abusive comments, the Returning Officer suggested that they could adjourn their press conference to a nearby car park as a compromise measure. Eventually this did happen, though with much bad grace.

Tensions often increase as polling day closes. At one parliamentary count in the West Midlands, the two mainstream candidates contesting the seat sat outside the counting hall in cars playing brinkmanship as to who would be the last to enter, presumably equating this with confidence in the result. Such tactics might be entertaining for some, but the Returning Officer agreed with the police that admittance to the count was only between certain hours to aid security – and these hours did not extend beyond midnight! The Returning Officer asked the agents where their candidates were and, eventually, with some reluctance was given this explanation. Being seriously unamused with this behaviour, the Returning Officer pointed out that he, on security grounds, might not admit these candidates at all and, in any event, he would proceed to read out the result in their absence or otherwise. There was no requirement for them to be present. A flurry of activity ensured and, continuing in this asinine vein, both candidates entered the hall together, although not speaking to each other. Both candidates are still MPs and have served/are serving as Ministers in the Government. At another parliamentary election in the East, a high profile media candidate completely declined the offer of attending the count and spent the whole evening with the "press pack", most of whom knew him personally. He was totally disinterested in the draft result (although his agent did cast an eye over the figures) and was only aware that he had saved his deposit when the final result was read out.

These two anecdotes represent levels of interest/disinterest at both ends of the spectrum. The bulk of candidates (and their counting agents) fall well within the median range of this spectrum and generally behave very well. Admittedly, there are horror stories of Returning Officers being assaulted both verbally and physically at the declaration of results, but these are rare instances indeed. Most candidates are entirely gracious in their speeches, whether victorious or defeated, inevitably thanking the Returning Officer and staff for their hard work. Arrangements for speeches are at the discretion of the Returning Officer and, frankly, at elections like the European and some Parishes there are far too many candidates for them all to make speeches. Some prior agreement with agents is needed, as is re-assurance that staff will not be offended if they do not receive public thanks from every candidate. Regrettably, over recent years, some Returning Officers have seen the need to prevent candidates with extreme views speaking after the declaration; indeed, in some places, no candidate, not even the successful one, has been allowed to speak to ensure equality of treatment. Television has recorded such scenes and some candidates have appeared with highly visible sticky tape over their mouths. None of this enhances the elections process and it is unfortunate that such steps have to be taken *in extremis*.

Campaign and publicity material

Queries often arise over the publicity that candidates put out during the election campaign. For instance, no campaign material may resemble a poll card but some is surprisingly similar and some leaflets model themselves on the ballot paper; some of these have actually been found inside ballot boxes, which says little for the aptitude of the voter but even less for the vigilance of the staff at the polling station.

The key point about campaign material is that it must contain an imprint with the full name and address of both printer and promoter, the latter term really covering the person who causes the material to be published.

The best plan for Returning Officers and their staff is to fervently avoid giving advice on this material. Leaflets, etc. are matters outside the statutory purview of the Returning Officer and his/her staff. Complaints should be directed to the police if agents/candidates think an offence has been committed and have evidence to substantiate their claim. The potential consequences of breaching these rules are severe – fines of up to £5,000. Nevertheless, informal queries can still arise regarding the suitability of email addresses or PO Box numbers within the imprint. For information purposes only, it is worthwhile knowing that they are both probably unsuitable as not being "proper" old style addresses, but without doubt both have been used in recent years. Should a website have an imprint address? The view of the Electoral Commission is that this would be good practice but what is the role of the internet service provider in such a case? They are hardly likely to know they are involved in the promotion of a particular campaign or point of view. These difficult points may eventually be tested in the courts. (For the purposes of the law of defamation, an internet service provider publishes a defamatory posting whenever a subscriber accesses a website to which that provider provides access.)

In a number of areas in Great Britain there are those involved with elections who believe posters are more trouble than they are worth. Although a minority view, there are localities where all the parties and independent candidates agree that they will not display posters, placards, etc. They firmly believe that the value of such advertising is limited, makes the environment look "tatty" and is difficult to remove as enthusiasm drains away from their supporters after polling day. (Posters must be removed within a fortnight of close of poll.)

Others take an entirely opposite view and are vigorous in their campaign to get posters in as many locations as possible. Problems sometimes arise when they are attached to street furniture such as lampposts and other directional signs. Remember these items are in the ownership of the local authority and the general rule is that consent to affix such items is withheld.

Those driving on motorways or other trunk roads may notice the more enterprising attempts to promote a particular party or candidate with large posters on farmers' trucks and trailers in fields adjoining the road. The display of these and other posters is controlled by the Town and Country Planning (Control of Advertisements) (England) Regulations 2007 where it does state in a schedule that "No advertisement shall be sited or displayed so as to endanger persons using any highway...". Practice in planning enforcement is variable in different parts of the country and, technically, motorways fall under the aegis of the Highways Agency, although other roads come under the control of the local Highways Authority.

Most commonplace is the poster on a board in a private garden or house window. Difficult issues sometimes arise when such a house or garden is adjacent to the polling station: school caretakers' houses, flats for wardens in sheltered schemes, the vicarage next to the Church Hall, etc. Some Returning Officers have had heated discussions with agents and candidates of other parties who want these posters removed but they are within private premises and, therefore, outside the Returning Officer's control. It is questionable whether they breach any service tenancy, but this is unlikely (they are not politically restricted posts at that level) and this is certainly not applicable to vicarages. It has been pointed out to certain candidates that throwing a brick through the offending window is straightforward criminal damage and a matter for the police. Similarly, it is also an offence to pay an elector to display posters or other advertisements unless it is a normal part of their business, e.g. an advertising agency.

Returning officer is not a referee

This chapter started by reflecting on the difficulties sometimes faced by Returning Officers when dealing with candidates who are also high profile members of their authorities. An important parallel point is that Returning Officers and their staff are not responsible for monitoring the conduct of candidates, agents and their supporters. The issue is clearly explained by the Electoral Commission in their guide for candidates and agents at the 2007 local elections:

> *"Where a candidate, agent or party worker has any concerns about the conduct of another person during the election campaign that could amount to electoral malpractice, if they are able to substantiate such a claim and are also willing to make a formal statement, the matter should be referred to the police. Allegations should not be made as a campaign tactic."*

The Returning Officer is not acting as a referee in a sports contest – thus, he has no power to disqualify a candidate for a false statement in a leaflet or, even, omission of the imprint. He has no formal disciplinary powers equating to red cards and sin bins. The test above reflects the fact that Returning Officers must act according to their statutory duties (and, on some occasions, their common law powers), however agitated the upset complainant may be; to be over-helpful may lead to serious repercussions.

Chapter 7

DEALING WITH THE MEDIA

"Television? The word is half Latin and half Greek. No
good can come of it" C P Scott

The Winchester experience

Picture the scene: a count at an old Guildhall in a charming Hampshire town in the 1997 General Election – could it be close? The Conservatives have held this seat almost as of right for more years than anyone can remember. The Returning Officer is experienced and highly competent with a strong elections team – and then calamity! A very close result turning on some 50 papers not being stamped with the official mark, though with a very narrow majority of those showing a clear intention to vote for the Conservative candidate but also some very unusual "rejected papers" which could be interpreted in a number of ways. The Lib Dems take the seat by a majority 2 or 3 – or do they? For with this level of closeness, the count is still going on some 16 hours after the close of poll! Tension is increasing, petitions are being threatened and local councillors who have known the Returning Officer for many years are now not speaking to him! What does all this add up to? – a great news story, whatever the rights and wrongs of the electoral process.

So on the evening of 1st May, Winchester had just two local TV stations, two local radio stations, hospital radio and journalists from three local newspapers. When the story, outlined above, started to break, the town was besieged with media crews and journalists – the street outside the Guildhall had to be closed to traffic as it was blocked by parked TV vans. The case arrived in the High Court but the contentious issues were settled by agreement outside a full formal hearing (legal costs, nevertheless, still ran into hundreds of thousands of pounds). A by-election was ordered to be run on 20th November.

How did the media react then? In force! On that day in November, the following press pack turned up:

> BBC Election Programme, BBC Breakfast News, Newsnight, ITN, Sky News, GMTV, BBC TV South, Meridian TV, BBC Radio 4 and 5, Radio Solent, Ocean FM, Cable Radio, Hospital Radio, Daily Telegraph, Times, Guardian, Independent, Evening Standard, Press Association, Solent News Agency, Fast News Photos, Southern Daily Echo, Winchester Extra, Hampshire Chronicle, Portsmouth News – about 100 journalists in all!

All these people with their different *modi operandi* had to be dealt with effectively by the Returning Officer and his staff, who already had a considerable task before them in running the election. On that occasion in 1997 the event passed off reasonably smoothly and the Liberal Democrats took the seat quite comfortably: a majority of some 20,000. But all this shows that the media have to be taken very seriously indeed and cannot be ignored. Most local authorities now have some specialist PR/communications staff and they should be employed in this task. The media have to be fed information or they simply set their own agenda in which Returning Officers/Electoral Administrators can often feature very unfavourably.

The Huntingdon experience

Most of the significant problems arise at the high profile counts. If the Prime Minister or senior Cabinet member is your MP then, inevitably, your constituency will receive massive press attention. It is simply essential to plan for this and the practice at Huntingdon (where PM John Major was the local MP in the 1990s) was to supplement the Council's usual press staff with some experienced administrative support – and preferably people with specialist electoral knowledge. Payment for this extra resource (and security) should be agreed with the (now) Ministry of Justice in advance; it is over and above the usual payments made for parliamentary constituencies.

Dealing with the Media

The Returning Officer at Huntingdon (the author) met as many media representatives as possible at the counting hall a couple of weeks before polling day – about 35/40 appeared, mainly from the BBC and other TV stations. The main message stressed to them was that this was a significant and challenging piece of work to undertake and the Returning Officer did not regard the event as entertainment for the masses. He was perfectly happy to co-operate with all the media who wished to attend (eventually some 250 from as far away as Japan) but they had to respect important matters like the integrity of the process and overall security. Fortunately, the Huntingdon count takes place in a very large sports hall (the size of six badminton courts) with a very generous balcony overlooking it – plenty of room for TV cameras and broadcasting equipment. Adjoining the counting room is one of the largest public halls in the county which can accommodate some 450 people (again with a balcony, a bar and separate entrances/exits). This second hall was to be a media HQ (they were charged a fee to cover the Council's costs). Outside is a huge car park with spaces for 500/600 cars.

Despite these apparent physical advantages, the Returning Officer's approach did not receive an overwhelmingly effusive welcome. Although many were apparently working for the BBC, there was a distinct lack of internal co-operation between their various reporters from local and national levels, radio and television; everyone wanted "to do their own thing". This could be tolerated to a certain point, but time and space (even at this large venue) is not infinite. A particular TV station (not the BBC) wanted to install hidden cameras in the entrance foyer and sports hall ceiling to observe the Prime Minister's body language. This request was refused by the Returning Officer as both intrusive and unreasonable for the smooth running of the whole event (removing and replacing ceiling tiles for cabling and equipment causes extensive disruption). The TV representatives were most unhappy at this decision and promised trial runs and even a right of veto to the Returning Officer if he did not approve the broadcast pictures. Neither parts of this offer were attractive enough to cause the Returning Officer to change his mind and unhappiness ensued – but the election went on.

Using the obvious disagreements within the BBC ranks, the Returning Officer "befriended" an independent freelance producer who was covering this outside broadcast for the Corporation; previously, he had covered the independence celebrations from Hong Kong. This producer made a number of helpful suggestions for lighting and siting the actual results declaration, organising the parking of all the TV/radio vans in the car park, etc. This was filling rapidly and a firm of scaffolders were now building camera gantries outside the main hall entrance so that the arrival of the Prime Minister's car could be clearly captured. The reporters and their entourages were now starting to irritate the local police, impeding access to the hall and parking their vehicles off site with no consideration for local residents. More problems arose when some reporters from a very popular daily tabloid were refused access permits (they applied too late) and said they would seek revenge by hiring a helicopter to "buzz" the hall. Clearly, the security services were unhappy with this; there were more negotiations involving electoral staff and access permits were eventually issued (all vetted centrally through both security and police records).

Those TV programmes that felt they were getting a poor position at the counting hall decamped to the polling station where John Major and his family voted. More vehicles and camera gantries appeared in the (fairly small) car park at Great Stukeley Village Hall. More arguments ensued about the Prime Minister's car convoy gaining access to the door. Several photographers (unaware of electoral law) said they would like pictures inside the polling station – more work here for electoral staff trying to explain why this was not possible.

The practical point to take from all this, like the Winchester case above, is that really it has nothing to do, *per se*, with the electoral process and, worse still, detracts from the actual work needed to run an efficient election. Staff and extra resources are really the only answer, combined with firm determination not to be harassed by the press. Without doubt, the two case studies described above are unusual. Most counts and polling stations will not receive this sort of attention but it is still worthwhile ensuring that the press receive co-operation and do not "get in the way". The count and the declaration are still regarded by many in the media as theatre and part of the fabric of this nation, so they will probably want some coverage. Many Returning Officers, when counting a good number of seats at local elections, get the results on to the Council's website as soon as practicable; this is a great boon for the overstretched local radio station who can obtain results quickly and, more importantly, without constantly ringing the Council.

At a recent London Parliamentary by-election, the Chief Executive/ Returning Officer took a very positive line – "it's a great opportunity to promote your Council and your Borough". At the count, with 7 camera crews and over 50 journalists present, they established a special media centre, with live news feeds and catering. A briefing pack on the Borough was distributed. During quiet moments through a long night, particular developments in the Borough were explained. Finally, for the all-important announcement of the result, the stage was "dressed" appropriately with displays presenting powerful images and key messages. It was never going to meet all communication objectives, but when else is local government the focus of so much *positive* attention? Sadly, the usual national tabloid stories of councils are entirely negative and feature new taxes on family barbecues from local bureaucrats who think this will stop global warming or the banning of hanging baskets as contravening Health and Safety legislation.

Relationships with the local media

Remember that at local level you will be dealing with the same media throughout the rest of the year and, whilst some authorities have quite dreadful relationships with their local press, that is no reason to be dilatory or awkward in providing them with election results. The press can be quite vicious to Returning Officers. Following some delays and problems at a local election count, the Returning Officer at a Borough in the Home Counties had his picture on the front page of a weekly local paper, already famously hostile to the authority, underneath the eye-catching headline "This man earns £80,000 pa and cannot count to 20". This occurred some years ago (as the salary level indicates) but there is no doubt over the venom of feeling here. Like many election issues, there was a lot more to this story than the headline indicates and the whole matter went to court – defamation was also involved. Settlements were eventually reached but all the main protagonists still serve as officers and members in the same Borough. Another very distinguished Chief Executive from a northern Metropolitan Borough (who went on to attain high office in SOLACE) reports similar and unhappy exposure arising from the 2004 all-postal elections. They had experienced terrible problems with the ballot packs ("just about every combination of possible error was found") and provided much local newspaper copy, including a front-page headline "RESIGN!" beside his photograph! Clearly, he took the insult seriously as he made a precautionary contact with his trade union representative.

Again, sometimes, the press feel they should have access to parts of the process that are closed to them; we have already noted the example of the polling station above. Some TV pictures are now broadcast showing the inside of polling stations (following the fashion of Europe and newly emerging democracies) but it is hoped that these are either "mocked up" or taken before the poll opens. Also, it is quite common for the press to enquire as to the progress of nominations before that process closes. They usually want to know whether a particular candidate is actually standing or what allegiance a recent "floor-crosser" now displays. These queries can only be answered once the statement is published – 24 hours after nominations have closed – and no information should be disclosed before then. This can be difficult as local reporters are often in and out of Town Halls speaking to both the staff and other candidates/agents. Moreover, reporters and TV crews have been known to turn up with some candidates when they bring in their nominations papers: they are not part of the process whatever their earnest protestations, usually along the lines of "the public have a right to know" – and they will in the fullness of time...

A more recent development in the national media has been to take a deep interest in the electoral process as not fit for purpose and open to corruption. Much attention has been given to postal voting over the last few years following the famous Birmingham case in 2005, arising from the 2004 elections. This type of reporting usually centres on the so-called abuse of postal voting (as lacking the security and control found in polling stations) and also problems arising from software/printing failures. The common theme portrayed is one of chaos and confusion with portentous, almost eschatological consequences. Here are some typical headlines from 2007:

"Our very democracy is now on trial" (*Daily Telegraph*, 18th January)

"Postal Voting is a giant fiddle" (*Sunday Times*, 21st January)

"Ministers ignore e-voting fraud warning" (*Times*, 2nd March)

"Vote-rigging reforms too late" (*Daily Telegraph*, 18th January)

The latter headline covers a report of a speech by Sir Alistair Graham at the 2006 National Elections Conference. Electoral integrity is considered elsewhere in this book, but one short quotation will give a flavour of the story:

"Postal voting on demand has brought the gravest threat to faith in British democracy and new laws to safeguard elections may be too little, too late, Britain's sleaze watchdog has cautioned.

Police have reported 342 cases of electoral malpractice to the Crown Prosecution Service since 2001, when Parliament gave everyone the right to vote by post, Sir Alistair Graham disclosed recently.

Vote-rigging is spreading across the country and the Government has done nothing to examine the real extent of cheating, the Chairman of the Independent Committee on Standards in Public Life said.

We cannot continue to base our electoral process on trust alone when it appears that this trust is plainly abused and risks loss of public confidence in our democratic system."

Without wishing to sound too cynical, these reports all focus on the bad news aspects of elections with no or very little positive content. A slightly more balanced view was taken by Peter Riddell writing in the *Times* of 19th January 2007. He pointed out that "our elections cannot be stolen or bought and remain clean by international standards. The main problems with our representative democracy lie elsewhere, in the disengagement of a more demanding public with Parliament." However, despite this slightly more robust view, the coverage in totality is clearly disheartening for those involved in the actual administration of elections and certainly would encourage no one to pursue a career in this field! The geographical extent of these problems could be exaggerated but the AEA took these issues particularly seriously and, in a report on the May 2007 elections, published in July 2007 described the following:

"Media intrusion

It is not unusual for the media to seek out problems associated with the elections and this has indeed been a regular feature since the problems encountered in Birmingham in 2004. This year the media swiftly latched on to the difficulties being experienced by ROs, particularly in the area of personal identifier checks, and the inability of software to undertake that process in many parts of the country. The AEA was mindful of the need to restrict scaremongering but found itself caught between real concerns being expressed by ROs and that of the DCA which, despite being aware of the problems, failed to recognise them and be positive about addressing them. There was also a lack of intervention by the Electoral Commission in maintaining a stance on the difficulties being experienced in electoral offices.

It was clear from the vast number of media enquiries made to AEA Officers and the eventual reporting of comments that the media were intent on generating a picture of real conflict between the Commission, DCA and those attempting to resolve the issues in electoral offices. Despite the fact that opinion was divided on a number of issues, as this report clearly demonstrates, the public perception was one of confusion. This does little to improve trust and participation in the democratic process."

This led them to recommend that the Electoral Commission, the Ministry of Justice and the Association of Electoral Administrators develop a media strategy panel. Whether that analysis is correct and what materialises remains to be seen. However, for anyone involved in the electoral process, clearly extra care is now needed when speaking to the press.

Back to Winchester

This chapter will conclude with our starting point, the Winchester by-election of 1977 and an unfortunate postscript for the then Chief Executive/Returning Officer, David Cowan. Following the case, David and his wife took a well-deserved break at a small town they know well in the south-west of France. As they drove into the town to start their holiday, he noticed that there was voting in a local election going on and he looked in at the Mairie to observe the process. On his return to Winchester he met the new local MP, referred to the incident, and made a comment about not being able to get away from elections. The MP expressed surprise, as he had also been on holiday in Acquitaine and had stopped in the same town on the same day on his way to a family short-break holiday and had also looked in at the local Mairie to see what was going on.

The MP mentioned this coincidence to a London press reporter and the story appeared in the political anecdote column of the *Evening Standard*. Although the two families had not met, a local newspaper columnist back in Hampshire picked up this extraordinary co-incidence and wrote a piece which suggested that this juxtaposition of the Returning Officer and the MP being in the same place in France on the same day indicated David's lack of neutrality, insinuating that it was indicative that the Returning Officer had shown partiality to the Lib Dems. David took legal action against the paper for defamation and secured significant damages (for his favourite charity) and expenses in an out-of-court settlement. David always says that his completely unfair treatment by the paper was compensated for at the subsequent by-election, for written on a ballot paper was:

"David Cowan is innocent"

David says he allowed the vote!

Chapter 8

MANAGING SUPPLIERS AND OUTSOURCING

"Election management has become heavily technology-reliant...there is a high dependence on third party contractors and suppliers...we continue to see authorities being led by their suppliers, rather than finding suppliers to meet their needs and the requirements of the legislation"
Electoral Commission Report on National Assembly for Wales Elections, 2007

Running an election is, in project management terms, a large and complex exercise. It is inevitable that some form of outside input is required, albeit that a few large authorities can limit this to an extent. Nevertheless, for the vast bulk of authorities seeking services from contractors, it is simply essential. Broadly, there are three major and common categories of outsider supplies to deal with:

1. Printers.

2. Software suppliers.

3. The Royal Mail (or, possibly, a private mail deliverer).

(It would be highly unusual for a local authority to go to an outside recruitment agency for staff, but possible if there were particular problems.)

Some of the contracts are simply to supply materials, e.g. ballot papers. However, a growing trend over recent years has been for these contracts to be extended to provide associated services, e.g. the dispatch of postal votes. At the outset, it is important to be clear what you, as Returning Officer or Electoral Administrator, want to achieve with these contracts as the private sector are not slow to press their salesmanship upon you at the start of the process. Decisions on the extent of contracts should be made well in advance, bearing in mind the size of the task ahead (combined elections are now commonplace and resource hungry) and internal resources available. Again, with the general increase in demand for postal votes and the limited time available for printing/dispatch, it is worth considering alternative methods rather than the traditional use of in-house staff. Many local authorities have outsourced their other traditional functions and do not have a large pools of staff to draw on at short notice to "stuff" envelopes. Remember, the electoral process has an unforgiving timetable that is set in stone (foot and mouth disease is exceptional; parliamentary elections can still continue now when an independent candidate dies) and changing postal vote dispatch from Town Hall staff to a private company at a day or two's notice is virtually impossible as well as asking for trouble.

Checking suppliers

There are other very significant and fundamental considerations to address with regard to managing outside contractors and possible outsourcing. Whilst outsourcing parts of the process is perfectly legal and possible, remember that, in law, the responsibility for ensuring compliance with all the statutory requirements still rests personally with the Returning Officer. This cannot be avoided and, whatever the circumstances, the duties and obligations for the proper conduct of the election remain with the Returning Officer. There are a number of corollary points that flow from this utterly key principle. Obviously, if you are employing a contractor to undertake electoral work, it is worthwhile being entirely satisfied as to their bona fides, efficiency and reliability. Previous experience of electoral work is probably essential (although some would disagree) and to be a "guinea pig" is not always a good idea, especially when things go wrong as they can do with spectacular results in the electoral world. The Electoral Commission advise taking up references on a contractor but this is, perhaps, a little over-formal: simple oral checks with colleagues are probably a better method and reputable firms are always pleased to supply the names of customers.

Of course, there may be circumstances when you do not have the time to do this. There were some horror stories in 2007 of printers going bankrupt or into liquidation before ballot papers were even printed, let alone delivered to the Council offices. The most worrying feature of these stories is that, apparently, the firms concerned were both reputable and reliable, checks having been made as advised above. Replacement printers had to be found at very short notice and, unsurprisingly, it was the smaller local firms that local authorities turned to, many producing very satisfactory results at short notice – they would get the contract again next year!

Checking and proper preparation is important in other respects. If things do go wrong further downstream and the Returning Officer ends up in the court, they can expect serious criticism if there is an obvious weak arrangement with an outside supplier that has been given little attention. Hindsight is a cruel and precise science which takes no account of "I thought they would be all right" or "I was busy working on our Local Area Agreement at that time in March". These excuses are hopelessly tepid in the witness box in the High Court. Moreover, the insurance company which, hopefully, is backing you in this case will take a pretty dim view of casual outside arrangements. It is not suggested that such arrangements would cause them to vitiate their policy and withdraw cover, but it might cause them to rethink their cover for the future and the size of their premiums. Insurance is dealt with elsewhere in this book, but it is far from straightforward when loss adjusters become involved (some insurance companies have tried to withdraw cover for postal voting in recent years as it poses too high a risk).

Procurement skills

Whether at Returning Officer or Electoral Administrator level, none of the foregoing mishaps will enhance your career – indeed, for some Chief Executives it is a strong contributory factor to it ending, especially if the election produces a change of controlling party or new leader. This leads on to the second key consideration which is that outside procurement and contract management is a skill in itself and not possessed by everyone at whatever level they may be in the local authority management structure. There should be no shame or disgrace in coming to this realisation, simply a clear determination to obtain some advice in this regard. Much progress has been made in the public sector in recent years in this area of work (not just local government) and many councils have procurement officers on their staff or, at least, access to some specialist advice. This is not a text on procurement and so exposition at length on this topic will not be pursued but it is certainly worthwhile taking advice on contractual terms dealing with variable pricing, delivery details, etc. This is doubly important in the electoral process as contractors need to understand that, ready or not, the election is on the first Thursday in May; the process will not admit of any delay. The Electoral Commission advise:

> *"It is vital for the statutory requirements and their implications to be fully explained wherever contractors are used, in order to avoid any misunderstandings later."*

The last clause of that quotation is probably well meaning but unlikely to provide a defence in law nor, probably, to the press and members in fact.

Printing issues

And so to some practical considerations. With regard to printing and postal vote distribution, a key issue that has emerged in recent years is the capacity of that industry (nationally) to be able to cope with a huge peak of work in the April preceding the May election.

Postal voting packs are complex to print and distribute, not to mention all the ballot papers for polling day. Again, quality control is a key issue, for incorrect numbering and addressing can cause huge problems. Without wishing to denigrate the printing industry unfairly, there are a number of firms who certainly over-promise and under-deliver. Sales promises of the previous year or even made at the AEA conference/ exhibition in the previous February soon disappear. Here are a couple of stories from 2007:

> *"We used outsource printing as we entered into a three year contract with them last year. We had major problems throughout the election with the printers. I received very little contact from our "project manager" and was given no guidance on where to send data, in which format and by what deadline.*
>
> *The candidates' proofing programme did not work and the job that should have taken less than two hours actually took the best part of two days to complete and still had errors on the ballot papers after completion.*
>
> *I was told in January that our printers would be located in Derby, I then found out in March that they were actually located in Leicester. I asked to visit the printers to proof the postal ballot packs and after chasing this several times I was told that I could visit them on Sunday 22nd April at 5.00pm. Fortunately I was informed just before I set off that they would not be ready on Sunday, however I did not then receive any information about when they would be ready from the printers, they were eventually ready to go on Wednesday 25th April.*
>
> *We were also due to receive the polling station ballot books on Friday 27th April, they did not arrive until Monday 30th April, the quality of the print was appalling and we were 4,000 ballot papers short for one ward. We had also ordered additional large ballot papers for each polling station, they too were missing. I informed the printers immediately about the missing papers, however the large ballot papers did not arrive until 3.30pm on Wednesday 2nd*

May. I tried several times to contact the printers regarding the still missing 4,000 ballot papers and by 7.30pm on Wednesday 2nd May had not had any information from them at all, this resulted in us having to print the missing ballot papers in-house and issue stamping instruments to the affected polling stations. I then learned on Thursday morning that they had actually delivered the missing papers at 8.30pm on the Wednesday evening although they had not contacted me to let me know.

We also discovered on election day itself that the postal proxy votes had gone to the elector's address instead of the postal proxy's address. This was because the elector's address was printed on the left-hand side of the page and the proxy's address was printed on the right-hand side; however the window on the out-going envelope is on the left-hand side.

In addition they changed the numbering on the polling station ballot papers which resulted in me having to re-do our entire ballot paper accounts and verification sheets. They also did the corresponding numbers lists for us which caused us three days' extra work as they sent each 100 numbers as a separate text file to be opened, converted to a word file then printed off. My biggest frustration with the printers throughout the entire election was the lack of communication from them and the frustration at not being able to contact them at critical times."

From another authority:

"For the first time the printing of all election material was undertaken by an external contractor to make it easier to project manage. The company selected had worked with the Council for a number of years on the printing of the canvass forms and telephone and internet registration. They have always been reliable and have a good reputation in the elections field.

In addition to the external printing of the postal vote stationery, it was decided that, due to the high number of postal voters – 12,299 – the issue of postal ballot packs (i.e. the postal vote envelopes containing all the stationery and the ballot paper for each voter) should also be outsourced in part to relieve pressure on staff resources. The company offered a full service which included the printing of the stationery, the printing of the ballot papers themselves and the issue of ballot packs to Royal Mail for delivery, which provided good value for money.

In the event, the company along with the majority of other print suppliers, experienced capacity issues which resulted in delays and errors for most authorities. The Council had a number of printing problems in particular on the postal ballot packs for the parish elections which resulted in nine staff from Democratic Services spending the whole of Wednesday 25th April correcting the printing errors and then finally issuing the ballot papers manually. This had a knock-on effect for the Elections Team in preparing other aspects of the election. Despite all the printing issues the postal ballot packs were despatched to voters a week prior to the election, only a couple of days behind schedule. Some local authorities experienced even more serious delays and failed to issue their postal ballot packs until a couple of days before the election (there are even unconfirmed stories about one authority in the Midlands issuing packs on polling day).

Officers are currently looking at joint procurement of printing services for future elections with the other neighbouring authorities with a view to being in a position to wield greater bargaining power and resulting in a greater level of protection for individual Councils."

Both these experiences are taken from internal reports (kindly made available to the author) and come from large authorities in the north-west of England. These stories are not untypical. The AEA report on the 2007 election contains some even more graphic descriptions, with elections staff contemplating suicide in the run-up to polling day or, if eventually eschewing that unattractive option, certainly considering retirement after May. Ironically, most of the authorities that avoided very serious problems (there are *always* some sort of issues in the electoral process) seemed to adopt the old-fashioned approach of using the little local printer who has no formal contract (forget three quotations for price!) but always turns up at close of nomination in the office able, virtually, to print a perfectly satisfactory ballot paper with little or no direction from electoral staff. These are small companies that will work over the Easter break – or other bank holiday – deliver papers personally early on the morning of the first postal vote dispatch and usually charge an entirely modest price. They may not have the sophisticated equipment and will certainly not be able to send out postal votes for you but in today's marketplace they are certainly worth retaining. It is bizarre for it appears to contradict all the previous advice set out above and from the Electoral Commission. Nevertheless, for a good number of authorities, these are effective and well-tried suppliers. In the West Midlands, there is a story of one printer who had a number of small and medium-sized authorities as his clients for electoral work and he became, over the years, quite knowledgeable in this field. So much so that, at one local election, when a particular Electoral Administrator was having problems at the close of nominations, it was the printer deciding whose name – and in what format – was appearing on the ballot paper! More worryingly still, he was not shy in recounting this experience to other electoral staff, particularly those from whom he thought he had learnt these principles. Happily, the elections went well and there were no serious repercussions.

The little printers can often feature in another way but with more unfortunate consequences. There is the common practice in the printing industry of sub-contracting work, especially at peak times such as elections. Some sub-contractors are clearly more competent or better supervised than others. One northern Metropolitan Borough was concerned about the delay in their ballot papers arriving and could not contact their printers over a weekend. Eventually, on the following Monday they did receive rather vague assurances that their papers were about to be delivered, but were surprised when they were brought by a farmer from the Derbyshire Dales in a somewhat agricultural truck! The enterprising farmer had printing machinery in his barns (with or without planning consent?) and had been sub-contracted to print these ballot papers. Quality control was unsurprisingly modest and there were some errors but (this was some years ago) nothing on the scale of some experiences in 2007.

Rather than simply rely on one printer, some authorities spread the work around to specialist firms who are often in different parts of the country. Thus the following table shows the print work distribution in an Eastern Region authority:

One-piece mailer for postal vote	— Company in Scotland
Ballot papers	— Company in Norfolk
Notices (elections, nominations, etc.)	— In-house
Standard forms	— From specialist (Shaw's)

Clearly there are pros and cons with this approach and some would argue it is more difficult to manage than simply relating to one supplier. However, if there were to be a failure of one supplier then, at least, other printing could go ahead and there would probably be a better chance of finding a replacement printer for a smaller part of the process at short notice, rather than a sizeable contract.

It is always worthwhile visiting the company if you have outsourced the distribution work to them.

Whatever their sales pitch, remember they are printers and not necessarily *au fait* with all of the subtleties of the electoral process. A few years ago, an authority in the Home Counties had an unpleasant experience when some 9,000 postal votes were dispatched without the official mark. By the time the discovery was made, they were into the postal system and not able to be retrieved. There was very serious trouble indeed at that Council and many votes were disallowed. Here are two recent examples from the 2007 local elections taken from the AEA report:

> *"We chose the 'fully managed' postal vote service provided by A which is the most comprehensive (and expensive) support they provide. It includes production and distribution of postal ballot packs, provision of scanning equipment to deal with the opening of postal votes and a Project Manager on site during the week of the elections. We also chose A to produce our ballot papers.*

> *By no means an exhaustive list, but the following is a list of some of the problems we have encountered:*

> ● *Lack of support and guidance throughout the process. We were led to believe that we would know who our Project Manager was weeks ago so we could work through the process together and get advice from him throughout the process. Instead we have been dealing with a variety of different people at A and the Project Manager was only assigned to us at the end of last week.*

> ● *Concerns that the form of Postal Voting Statement does not follow the wording prescribed in the Local Elections (Principal Areas) Rules 2006 for combined elections. When we queried this with the company we were told there was nothing we could do about it as the Postal Voting Statements were already with the printers.*

- *The company not meeting deadlines they had set. For example, they had stated that all ballot paper proofs would be with us by 11th April and yet there are still some we are waiting for. We have been given various false promises during the last week or so as to when we would receive them.*

- *Where we have made amendments to proofs the company has not picked them up and have sent back to us proofs with the same errors not rectified.*

- *We have left numerous messages with one of our contacts at A and he has failed to respond at all.*

You can imagine the frustration that we are feeling and the problems that this has caused us at what is obviously an already pressurised and critical time for us.

The problems have also been exacerbated by failures in software from L/B and delays caused by waiting for these issues to be resolved."

From the second authority:

"We are in a similar position we also decided to have the fully managed Postal Vote Service offered by A. We were promised that our postal vote packs would be ready for us to check on Sunday 22/04/07 at ****** in ******* and then be returned to *****. On arriving in ***** I was told that there was nothing for me at ***** on Tuesday. Today I have been informed that they are now putting contingency plans into operation and they are sending the postal votes to ***** to be packed and we should get them hopefully Tuesday afternoon or Wednesday morning more likely. I was intending to post them today but looks like it will be Wednesday at the earliest if I am lucky.

I should also add that we had hoped that the postal votes would be sent out by A on Monday at the latest. Due to considerable problems with the quality of the printing this has been delayed and the postal votes are now expected to be posted this evening.

The quality of the printing of the ballot papers has not been of the required quality which has resulted in many of the samples taken to be rejected by the scanner. This problem has taken almost one week to reach the position where we have now issued instructions for the postal papers to be printed. We dare not delay any further in case we are accused of disenfranchising any voter.

Further tests will be carried out on Thursday to check the quality of the papers to be issued to polling stations."

The Royal Mail

Although some authorities use their own staff to deliver poll cards and postal votes, the Royal Mail return the latter. Over recent years, their performance has certainly improved and contacts between the Electoral Commission, the AEA, SOLACE, DCA (as was) and senior officials from the Royal Mail have established significantly better working relationships. There still needs to be close liaison at grass roots level between electoral administrators and individual Royal Mail managers to deal with particular issues, but there is much more support and interest in this work at national level from Royal Mail than in the past.

Unfortunately, threats of strikes do appear (October 2007, for instance) and sometimes materialise within the electoral timetable; this does lead to some disruption in service. Royal Mail maintain that their managerial staff can provide a level of service, though this has never been tested in the context of national elections. Would a strike and delayed return of postal votes affect the electoral timetable? Should a Returning Officer allow more time for postal votes to be returned? The answer to both questions is emphatically in the negative. Here is an extract from an opinion by Tim Straker, QC presented at a seminar in 2003:

> *"In respect of litigation before an election, enormous care is required because the opportunity for things going seriously wrong is greater than normal. First, everything will happen in a rush. Second, people inexperienced in elections may come to be involved. For example, printers who fail to appreciate the importance of marks on papers or postmen who fail to appreciate that they are playing a part in the process. Third, any litigation may well occur before a judge hearing the case in a hurry and with limited experience of electoral law. He may be looking for a solution between two parties, say the Returning Officer and a candidate or between two candidates, in a way which overlooks the other candidates or the public interested. Further, he may even be suffering from a curious delusion that litigation can cure all ills.*

> *A recent potential illustration happened in a recent Inner London authority by-election. This was clearly affected by the recent postal dispute. A candidate from a major party secured, I was told, an opinion to the effect that the Returning Officer could simply put back the close of the poll to accommodate the chance that as time passed the dispute might end and more postal votes be returned. On the face of it there is a superficial attraction in saying the time can be expanded but when one reflects on the precise timetable given by the rules and the danger of a discretionary decision favouring one side a realisation should be gained that the timetable cannot be changed."*

To garner up all the postal votes, "sweeps" of sorting offices just prior to close of poll have become fashionable (and expensive?) recently. Sometimes the Returning Officer personally (or a deputy) will appear, plus staff, at the local office (or offices) to collect in the last postal votes. There are other Returning Officers who feel differently and take the view it is up to the Royal Mail to deliver to the Council offices in the usual way. Sweeps are resource intensive and are not compulsory; it is a matter of local choice.

Election software

Software is an integral part of the electoral process now and its significance is growing. All Returning Officers and their staff are heavily reliant on software programs to produce the register, poll cards, postal voting lists, etc. The days of performing these tasks manually are long gone and, except in appalling moments of crisis, will not be returning. Some councils have developed their own systems but most rely on the four or five main suppliers. The major contemporary and highly contentious issue is the checking of personal identifiers for postal vote security which was first used in the local elections of 2007. This caused huge and well-publicised problems – systems not working, introduced too late, running repairs ("patches") only installed on polling day, reversion to manual checking, etc. One major company was called in to see the DCA as a result of complaints from local authorities. The situation was far from happy at virtually every election in 2007 and many authorities only got their IT software to work because they deployed internal resources to help – some of the suppliers were simply not delivering. Here is a typical experience taken from the AEA report:

- *System not as demonstrated – To coin a phrase from another user about the software supplier "They are making it up as they go along" despite input from users.*

- *System not installed until 14th February.*

- *At this point it came as a shock that it was to be internet based, i.e. no local scanned images.*

- *New scanner delivered – 16th February – sourced through software company – broken! They would not believe it to be broken – so requested an engineer to confirm.*

- *Replacement scanner provided – jammed after every 1/2 scans. Software company suggested it needed "wearing in – after 10,000 scans it would be okay" – then said "20,000"!*

- *Not happy software company send a representative down for almost three days to scan our forms – on day three confirmed that something must be wrong with the scanner.*

- *Engineer calls – yes the sensor is broken.*

- *We struggled through and scanned in all our forms.*

- *In between all this – the company could not process our scanned images so we had to use a hand held bar code reader to scan forms into notepad for processing at the company.*

- *A data file was returned to update our system – to enable us to post out reminders. Came in over a weekend to undertake this task – scanning in 19,000 forms!*

- *No real written instructions provided from the company or updates as to progress. Difficult getting replies to emails, requests and messages left at the company.*

- *The company managed eventually to process our forms – well so they say.*

- *Getting updated data from the company for the cancellations was like getting blood out of a stone.*

- *Consequently reminders were late – affecting the candidate/ agent printing of AV lists and posting of poll cards, etc.*

- *Still waiting for the company to provide information on scanning/linking in non bar-coded forms! Postal verification starts next Tuesday!*

- *Apparently for processing the voting statements we will be provided with passwords and log in information to enable the*

*system to work. We have also been promised "INSTRUCTIONS"
wow.*

- *Suffice to say we have back-up plans – albeit of a manual
  nature. There are a number of issues relating to software that
  the company cannot provide and they "may be able to provide
  next year".*

At the time of writing, it can only be hoped that the situation improves.
To run a General Election on this basis would be horribly and unfairly
testing to all staff.

Chapter 9

ELECTORAL INTEGRITY

"Is electoral fraud 'very rare' in Britain, as the Department for Constitutional Affairs still insist? Or should we believe Richard Mawrey QC, the judge in the infamous Birmingham vote rigging case of 2005, that the government is 'in denial' about standards of conduct in British elections – especially local elections – that 'would disgrace a banana republic'?...

"The introduction of postal voting on demand has undoubtedly made it much easier to fiddle votes"
Sunday Times, 21st January 2007

"...we can no longer base our electoral system on trust alone if we wish to protect the integrity of our electoral system...Since the introduction of postal voting on demand there has been a growing perception that the electoral system is more susceptible to organised electoral fraud"
Committee on Standards in Public Life, 2007

"For 2007 the Electoral Commission's general impression to date is that the volume and scale of offences are both considerably down on 2006. There is no instance of an allegation anywhere near the scale of Tower Hamlets (2006), Bradford (2005), Peterborough (2004) or Birmingham (2004). This is notable given the larger number of elections this year (well in excess of 300)...The low level of reports and allegations of offences this year is encouraging" Electoral Commission Report on Local Government Elections in 2007

So what is the true picture? Can a universal truth as a secure mooring be formulated to describe the integrity of our elections? More to the point, for this text, what should those charged with the running of elections be doing about all this?

The only really unchallengeable and firm universal truth is that no one knows! Many have very strong views as the quotations above indicate but this is an issue that is impossible to quantify accurately. The problem is similar to the contentious matter of criminal statistics generally which fluctuate up and down – do they really reflect a true drop in the increase/decrease of criminality or simply the awareness and reporting of crime? The related problem with criminal statistics is their constant reclassification, although that does not really apply in the electoral field where most of the current offences still date from the Victorian era. Has electoral fraud always been in our system to some extent and is only now being reported? Has the change to postal voting on demand exacerbated the position? Has the introduction of postal vote personal identifiers driven some fraud out of the system? No-one has produced definitive answers to these questions (though the Electoral Commission has welcomed the improved security of postal voting) and, frankly, for the foreseeable future no-one is likely to either.

Responding to possible fraud

So what can and should be done in practical terms? Of course, many Returning Officers will see no evidence whatsoever of deliberate fraud throughout their whole careers, but some have it as a continuous problem. The perception is that of a concentration in certain inner city areas and certain minority groupings, but even this can be successfully disputed. Sir Alistair Graham, whilst Chairman of the Committee on Standards in Public Life, was always at great pains to point out cases in the leafy shire districts – Havant (2002), Guildford (2003) and Woking (2006) are listed in the schedule printed in the report produced by his committee which reviewed the overall work of the Electoral Commission.

There is no shortage of advice on the topic emanating from the Electoral Commission, both for Returning Officers and police forces, the latter being published jointly with ACPO (February 2007). The practical starting point is that Returning Officers should refer allegations of electoral fraud or malpractice to the police for investigation. Returning Officers are not detectives and should not take it upon themselves or instruct their staff to usurp this law enforcement role. Besides which, all electoral staff will be very busy with a multitude of other demanding tasks at this stage in the process and really do not have the time or resources to mount a detailed probe. However, it is only fair to record that many senior police officers complain at the high volume of allegations referred to them, many being entirely trivial (little more than a clash of personalities, they state) and totally without foundation. Accordingly, it would seem reasonable for the Returning Officer or Electoral Administrator to say to the angry candidate or agent that they are quite at liberty to pursue their complaint with the police but, *prima facie*, it would appear that no offence has been committed. The Electoral Commission also have designated staff to advise Returning Officers and their staff on the handling and referral of electoral malpractice allegations. The Electoral Commission have agreed a revised code of conduct with the political parties on the handling of postal vote applications and postal ballot papers; in their report on the 2007 local elections, the Commission record several instances of non-adherence to this code (entirely voluntary) which they pursued with the political party concerned. For future years, they intend to produce a pocket-sized quick guide to the code that can be referred to by party activists on the ground during the campaign period. A pocket guide for police officers has already been produced; it gives general practical advice on electoral administration.

Postal voting problems

SOLACE has expressed some serious reservations about the postal voting code. The Society believes that party workers should, in no circumstances whatsoever, be involved in returning completed postal ballots and that the national code is too weak in this respect – paragraph 19 effectively allows the party representative to take this type of vote back to the Town Hall. Indeed, there are some Returning Officers who would go further and seek to stop party workers handling postal vote applications but, in the context of low turnouts, this is considered a step too far by most. In some areas, local protocols have been agreed that, for instance, seek to prevent party workers handling postal votes: Kettering and Southampton are good examples. This is a difficult issue as most of the allegations of electoral impropriety emanate from the parties themselves against their opponents and, until they either agree to this total ban (or achieve some other form of staff regulation), problems will arise. For their part, the parties dispute the claim that Returning Officers are efficient enough to send out staff at short notice to collect postal ballots (most Returning Officers report very few elderly or immobile people requesting such assistance) and, in any event, their workers know the elderly postal voters well, enjoying their trust as friends, neighbours or relatives. This issue will rumble on, being unlikely to feature in legislation.

Police involvement

Police awareness of electoral integrity has improved dramatically over the last few years. Forces are advised to establish a Gold Command structure for the entire election process and, also, have a "SPOC" – Single Point of Contact. This person will be the key link for the police with all the other stakeholders in the process, attending pre-election planning meetings with local authority staff. Again, it is recommended that the SPOC should attend and give input to any candidate and election agent briefing by the Returning Officer and electoral staff (usually in April). Another Electoral Commission/ACPO suggestion for areas with universities/colleges is that the force student liaison officer should offer to assist the Returning Officer in making the delivery of postal votes to multi-occupied student properties more secure by raising awareness of security issues and identifying key contacts who are prepared to take responsibility for ensuring the postal ballots are delivered to the intended recipients.

Police presence at polling stations is much more restricted these days and probably limited to a brief call at some stations. The guidance recommends that in areas of high risk, consideration should be given to escorting the transfer of ballot boxes from polling stations to the count, as well as to overnight security of boxes if the count is on Friday morning. Many years ago, police presence for these parts of the process was more prevalent. At one northern Borough, the Town Clerk had no confidence in the reliability of cars owned by polling staff and insisted on ballot boxes being brought to the count in a taxi with a police escort! This practice would certainly be regarded as entirely excessive in the 21st Century!

Extra anti-fraud measures?

Can the Electoral Registration Officer/Returning Officer take steps outside the strict statutory boundaries of their respective roles in the interests of ensuring the integrity of the system? Although not tested in the courts, the view of leading counsel is a clear "no". Thus, at one authority, there were particular concerns over personation and the Returning Officer considered positioning additional staff, over and above the usual Presiding Officer and Poll Clerks, in polling stations with a view to identifying and challenging repeat voters or those involved in personation. Leading counsel advised against this, pointing to the Local Elections Rules which provide for a series of questions which may be asked of persons applying as electors or proxies. Save as authorised by rule (i.e. those particular questions), no inquiry shall be permitted as to the right of any person to vote. Further, a person must not be prevented from voting by reason only that a candidate or his agent declares he has reasonable cause to believe personation is being committed or the person is arrested for personation.

At the same Authority, the Chief Executive acting as Electoral Registration Officer had serious concerns about bulk applications for inclusion on the register of electors. There had been a significant influx of people from Eastern Europe (the new accession states to the European Union), many of whom were living in houses in multiple occupation (HMOs). The Council had received information which suggested that some of the applications for registration were far from *bona fide*. It appeared that the owners or managers of HMOs were collecting a number of completed registration forms from the occupiers and then forwarding them to the Electoral Registration Officer. In all instances, the applications were apparently supported by evidence of employment and/or residence at the property in question. A data matching exercise was carried out and the results showed:

a) in some instances, the level of occupation of the properties was higher than the size of the property suggested was reasonable;

b) there were some instances of duplicate applications, including applications in circumstances where an individual was already on the register;

c) where there were duplicate applications, the information provided was inconsistent in that signatures did not match and/or the date of moving into the property differed.

Counsel's advice was also sought on the circumstances in which the Electoral Registration Officer can reject such applications for registration and the evidence which would be required to support such a rejection. Again, would the Returning Officer (the same person as the Electoral Registration Officer) be justified in intervening to prevent people seeking to vote in an effort to prevent personation and other electoral fraud occurring? Counsel took the view that the Registration Officer's powers are circumscribed by the Act and regulations. This means that the potential points for requesting evidence or information are nationality and age and the sufficiency of the particulars of the application. His advice continued:

> "If any doubts about age or nationality have been overcome and particulars supplied as required under Regulation 26, whether initially or subsequent to a request, then Registration must follow. This could be so even if the material was inconsistent with information held for other purposes (e.g. benefits or Council Tax). Rejection of an application can occur if the registration officer considers that the particulars have not been provided or that the requirements for age or nationality are not met.
>
> Removal from the register is statutorily controlled and can only occur in accordance with the relevant legislative provisions. Thus by Section 10(A)(5) (subject to Section 10A(5A) of the 1983 Act) where the name of a person is duly entered in a register in respect of any address the elector is entitled to remain registered in respect of that address until such time as the registration officer determines, on the conclusion of a canvass under Section 10, either that the elector was not registered on 15th October for the year in question; or the form mentioned in Section 10(4) was not returned; or for any other reason insufficient information was obtained as to whether the elector was resident at that address and the registration officer is unable to satisfy himself that he was; or determines in the prescribed circumstances that the elector has ceased to be resident at that address so as to satisfy the conditions for registration. It will be appreciated that the trigger for removal from the register is the canvass not an application to be registered.
>
> Under the same heading the question is asked whether the Returning Officer would be justified in intervening to prevent people from voting in an effort to prevent personation or other electoral fraud occurring. However, the role of a Returning Officer is constrained by the terms of the legislation. He does not have a general remit to

seek to prevent personation or electoral fraud. A Returning Officer should not intervene save in those very limited circumstances laid down in the Principal Area Rules, i.e. the Local Elections (Principal Areas) (England and Wales) Rules 2006, S.I. 2006 No. 3304."

As events unfolded at this authority, some problems were encountered; the most blatant was a case of personation whereby a man (originally from Poland) attempted to vote using a polling card in the name of an Asian woman. Assurances were given to him by the organisers of this "scam" that the polling staff would not notice as they did not understand these names; however, they did. He was apparently paid £25 and claimed that he was simply one of a number doing this. He was arrested (a police constable was present at the polling station) with two others and charged; a successful prosecution ensued.

Finally, mention should be made of an intervention by the Parliamentary Assembly of the Council of Europe investigating alleged electoral fraud in the United Kingdom. The Council appointed two rapporteurs (from Germany and Poland) to investigate and they visited the UK in February 2007, interviewing a number of people including the author. At the time of writing, a final report from them had yet to be published.

Chapter 10

PETITIONS

"...fresh from brawling courts
And dusty purlieus of the law" Tennyson

Election results, whether local or parliamentary, can only be challenged in law by way of election petition which is a very technical and complex process through the High Court. At a recent private meeting at the Electoral Commission, several distinguished QCs described the process as even more complex than usual High Court litigation which, frankly, for the non-specialist layman is already a minefield! Thus, this text will not try to describe all the technical rules but seek to relate some practical advice and experience.

Howsoever construed, petitions are not good news for the Returning Officer. Whether they arise through neglect or an error made in good faith or the action of a member of staff of which the Returning Officer had no knowledge, they do not make for a happy ending to the electoral process. They are usually launched against a background of local recrimination and unpleasantness in the local media which, at best, is very distracting and, at worst, very destructive of the individual. Some arise to challenge the result which has been declared in error due to some simple mathematical fault or double counting, etc. The petition is the only way to challenge and change the result, even if the Returning Officer admits fault and decides not to defend the action. Insurance companies (covering the Returning Officer) are always anxious to mitigate their losses and limit their exposure to substantial costs in the High Court so it would be usual in such circumstances to end proceedings as swiftly as possible. In 2006, a case of this type arose in Birmingham when the incorrect result was announced due to double counting and the BNP candidate was duly elected. Eventually, in August 2006, the High Court ruled this an error and declared that the Labour candidate should in fact be the elected member in that ward.

A retired Chief Executive in the West Country recalls a count at an early stage in his career when he realised, later in the evening, he had already declared a result that was incorrect. Rather boldly, he spoke to the candidates and agents concerned, re-read the result with the correct figures and they all accepted the new outcome after this unusual process. Unsurprisingly, with these powers of persuasion, he pursued a very successful career as a Chief Executive (eventually in a major London Borough and as National Secretary of SOLACE) but thereafter always checked results carefully before reading them out at the count!

Several experienced Returning Officers and lawyers have argued that cases such as this should be covered by a much simpler, virtually administrative, procedure. Thus, if it is obvious to all concerned that an error has been made then, surely, a simple application to a judge in chambers could be made to amend the result, ensuring that the candidate with the most votes is duly elected. Such a different process would require new primary legislation – which makes it highly unlikely in the near future – as well as agreement from the major political parties. If enacted, the actual application would require support from all parties involved in that particular case, but it would certainly be a more expeditious and efficient process than the election petition.

The County Court alternative

Another process sometimes used in local elections is to involve the County Court in an inspection of documents (Rule 53 of the 2006 Local Elections Rules). The most common set of facts to support these referrals is the finding of uncounted votes (usually postal) after the result has been announced. At the bottom of some box or behind a pile of papers, someone finds a large packet or envelope full of postal votes.

Could they affect the result? How many people know of their existence? More to the point, what should the Returning Officer do now? There are apocryphal stories of these papers mysteriously finding their way to a nearby shredder or unofficial recounts taking place, sometimes even with the agents/candidates present, all sworn to secrecy and agreeing to honour a "revised" result. Although some of these stories may be exaggerated in their retelling late at night in the conference hotel bar, there is more than a grain of truth to some. Of course, none can have any formal approval, for the correct process would either be for the result to be challenged in a petition or application made to the County Court for an inspection of these papers. The County Court process is much quicker than the High Court, but the vital practical point is for the Returning Officer and staff to get legal advice as soon as possible whenever facing these circumstances; contact with the insurance company is also worthwhile. Remember, all the major political parties have retained lawyers (firms of solicitors in Central London) who will not be slow to contact the local authority Returning Officer, often in a most unsympathetic way. Here is an example from Gerald Shamash (of Steel and Shamash), acting for the Labour Party and quoted in the *Times* in May 2001:

> *The low point, Shamash says, was in Halifax, where a man tried to stand as Alice Mahon, the name of the Labour candidate. "I phoned the Returning Officer and said 'You cannot allow him to stand as Alice, he's a man'. The Returning Officer said 'I do not know if you are old enough to remember but there was a pop star called Alice B Cooper' I said 'Is that your best point?' and that was the end of that'."*

The parties also use specialist Counsel. Sue Dixon, of Penningtons for the Conservatives, said in the same article:

> *"Electoral law has its basis in the House of Commons procedures, so it is not normal litigation."*

Piers Coleman of Nicholson, Graham & Jones (advising the Liberal Democrats) adds on this point:

"What is and is not valid is surprisingly arcane."

These quotations serve simply to underline the earlier point that specialist legal advice is essential at an early stage. Again, when supported by an insurance company they usually (though not invariably) like to appoint their own lawyers, preferably at an early, rather than later, stage.

An important defence

However, not all mistakes in the process lead directly up The Strand to the High Court. Derived from the common law and now contained in statute, there is an important rule that if an error occurs or there is departure from the process, the result will not be vitiated if:

a) the rest of the electoral process was conducted substantially in accordance with the law; and

b) the error or departure did not affect the result.

The other derivative corollary from these principles is that if the election was conducted so badly that it could never be considered as substantially in accordance with the law, the result will be vitiated whether or not the result was affected.

These are highly important and useful principles. Indeed, if, in both fact and law, they can be established by a Returning Officer as early as possible against any potential threats of a petition, then it is fair to say that the petition may not run against him/her. However, it is always worth considering these principles as a shield, not a sword. It would be fatal, for instance, to deliberately short cut proper electoral procedures on the basis that the result will not be affected (large winning majorities, etc.) and the rest of the process is pretty much in line with the law. It is submitted that the court would take an unsympathetic attitude to such a scenario; the idea behind these rules is to protect the *bona fide* error, often made by someone other than the Returning Officer in a stressful moment.

So how do the courts apply these principles in practice? In a 1974 case (*Gunn v Sharp*), Stephenson LJ said:

> *"For an election to be substantially in accordance with the law there must be a real election by ballot and no such substantial departure from the procedure laid down by Parliament so as to make the ordinary man condemn the election as a sham or a travesty of an election by ballot. Instances of such a substantial departure would be allowing voters to vote for a person who was not in fact a candidate or refusing to accept a qualified candidate on some illegal ground or disenfranchising a substantial proportion of qualified votes."*

Other cases give an indication of irregularities that resulted in elections being declared void and those that did not. Care must be taken with some of the old cases for, as long as 30 years ago, judges like Lord Denning were criticising some of the 19th Century decisions, casting doubts on their applicability to the contemporary world. Nevertheless, the following examples are gleaned from 19th, 20th and 21st Century case law.

Elections declared void

- Improper refusal by Returning Officer to include validly nominated candidate.

- Incorrect calculation of time – candidates and large numbers of electors misled as to proper closing date for nominations and date of poll.

- At an all-postal (pilot scheme) local election, ballot papers were sent out to electors containing the names of candidates for the wrong ward (printers admitted error but this did not absolve the Returning Officer).

- Failure of two polling stations to open at all – large number of voters not able to exercise franchise.

Elections not declared void

- Contradictory notices as to how many candidates votes may be given for – one said for one candidate only, another said could vote for up to two.

- Failure of Presiding Officer to show the ballot boxes empty before opening of poll.

- Returning Officer refusing recount – a subsequent count ordered by the court found original result to be correct.

- Polling station opened 45 minutes late due to unforeseen accident.

The foregoing can only be a summary of lengthy cases and, at the end of the day, it is up to the court to decide on the basis of the evidence submitted as to the applicability of the two-part "Saving" rule.

Petitions must be presented within 21 days after polling day and the petitioner (the person/persons starting the petition) must give security for costs – in layman's terms, make a payment into court. For parliamentary petitions this is up to £5,000 (as the court directs), £2,500 for local elections and £1,500 for parish/community elections. There has been some recent debate as to whether these figures are too high or too low – unsurprisingly, many Returning Officers would like to see them increased considerably to deter litigants, but others (often aggrieved independent candidates) think the figures too high and a barrier to justice. Of course, if a case proceeds, then the costs involved would be many times higher than this.

Petitions

There are not huge numbers of petitions launched each year. The Electoral Commission monitor the level and type of petition from year to year. Thus, in 2006, eight petitions were lodged following the May local elections (over 170 in number):

- Two petitions relating to inaccurate counts were upheld and the petitioners declared duly elected.

- Three petitions were struck out for failure to follow the proper procedure.

- Two petitions were struck out because no evidence proving the corrupt practice prevailed was presented.

- One petition relating to an ineligible candidate on the grounds of employment was upheld and the election declared void.

In 2007 (some 312 elections), seven election petitions were issued:

- Birmingham City Council

- Burnley Borough Council

- Leicester City Council

- Slough Borough Council

- South Holland District Council (resolved quickly as it related to an inaccurate count and the petitioner was declared elected)

- South Tyneside Metropolitan Borough Council

- Southsea Town Council.

Most Returning Officers will not, thankfully, experience a petition throughout the entire course of their career. Often threats are made at the count in the heat of the moment but, with the passage of a couple of days, tempers cool and the attractiveness of lengthy, expensive proceedings in the High Court invariably diminishes.

Chapter 11

INSURANCE

"Oh, dry the starting tear,
for they were heavily insured..." W S Gilbert

Insurance is simply essential for any Returning Officer running any election – there can be no departure from this utterly golden rule. The couplet above (from a poem, not a Savoy opera) refers to ship owners who were not disappointed to see their cargoes sinking as they would profit handsomely from the insurance payout. Similar considerations do not, however, apply in the election field. With most modern policies, encounters with insurance companies are often complex and trying, whether or not in the field of elections.

The standard policy and local variations

The usual position is that Returning Officers and election staff are covered by insurance policies from their employing authorities – this applies to local and Westminster parliamentary elections. Most local authorities have the standard Zurich Mutual policy with this cover but some other Councils have gone out to the insurance market and found more competitively priced policies. There is nothing wrong with this so long as adequate cover is obtained and it is essential that Returning Officers check their own individual position in their authority. There are examples where a substantial excess of £100,000 has been added to a general policy, thus reducing the annual premium with the Council bearing the risk up to that amount. For electoral purposes this is useless to the Returning Officer and offers worthless protection to cover, for instance, costs in the High Court. The view of experienced Returning Officers is that the best excess is nil and suitable arrangements should be made to achieve this with the insurance company.

The cover sought should be extensive. Most Returning Officers generally think in terms of cover if facing an election petition, but other situations arise too. Thus, the Returning Officer as an employer may face a claim from staff who injure themselves whilst on duty at the polling station. The stories of such claims are legion – trips on steps, assault by an elector, damage to clothing from dangerous radiators, etc. It is often tempting to ask precisely what the staff were doing to incur such harmful misfortune, but wiser counsel of ignorance should probably prevail. In any event, some claim is likely to materialise that should be dealt with by the insurers; have electoral staff some sort of process for handling this? Considerations include that a claim form will be required; the possiblility of an excess to cover administrative costs (£50 to £100 not unusual); what evidence the insurers require, etc.? All these and other issues arise which are outwith the general core business of electoral staff, often, at this stage, tired and trying to clear up after a very demanding election. Arguments with insurance companies and angry staff do not enhance this process but are sometimes inevitable.

There are always some situations not covered by insurance – criminal acts, gross negligence and utter recklessness are simply standard to all policies. There was a claim once in a northern seaside authority of someone (employed by the Council) who claimed that he was "promised" a Presiding Officer job on polling day but later, for horribly complex reasons, was not so appointed. He tried to claim for loss of earnings against the insurers (not discouraged by the Council in question who were rapidly tiring of this person) but that came to naught. Proceedings in the County Court were contemplated but, fortunately, eventually struck out.

Another classic and very common area for problems is vehicle insurance. The number of large 4x4 vehicles which manage to clip their wing mirrors or scratch their doors on 19th Century school gate posts is staggering. The staff claim this was the only safe parking place and convenient to load up all the boxes, packages, etc. at 10.00pm, but these Victorian entrances were not designed for "Chelsea Tractors"! The general position on virtually all election insurance is that claims such as these are not covered and must be pursued by the owners' individual policies. This leads to much complaining about loss of no-claims bonus, increased premiums, etc. but the Returning Officer and staff should resist involvement as firmly as possible. A City Council in the east had so much trouble with these claims that they used to ask Presiding Officers to bring in their car insurance policies to be checked before their appointment was validated. Some policies – particularly for the numerous polling day staff who are now retired – exclude business use and would therefore not be applicable to election appointment. It must be said that many regard car insurance checking as wildly "over the top" in the midst of trying to run an election and this text would not recommend such a course of action.

European elections

The position with European elections has always been outside the mainstream local authority policies. For both the 1999 and 2004 elections, a block policy was obtained to cover Regional Returning Officers, Local Returning Officers and their staff. The premium was paid for by the then responsible Central Government Departments (Home Office and DCA). Obtaining this cover in 2004 was particularly difficult as the insurance business, highly cognisant of fraud and postal voting scandals, does not regard this as an attractive risk. The 2004 policy attracted a hefty six-figure premium and was eventually underwritten by an American company. For the 2009 European election it is virtually certain that no policy will be forthcoming and electoral staff will be looking for an indemnity from the Ministry of Justice. This has been fairly recognised by officials in the Electoral Policy Division at the time of writing. They point to Returning Officer guidance for both the last European and Westminster parliamentary elections that clearly indicates support with a sympathetic willingness to grant an indemnity:

> *"The (then) DCA are prepared to indemnify Regional Returning Officers and Local Returning Officers against claims by injured*

employees for compensation falling outside the industrial injuries scheme, provided that the Regional Returning Officer is not personally to blame. The DCA will also indemnify Regional Returning Officers and Local Returning Officers against claims which may be made against them in their official capacity in respect of personal injuries to third parties and in respect of fire or damage to premises used for election purposes, subject to reasonable care having been taken to prevent accidents and damage.

Home Office Circular RPA 388 dated 9th June 1994, para 3, further clarified that it is unnecessary for Regional Returning Officers and Local Returning Officers to take out insurance to cover the cost of an election petition at which it was successfully alleged that the election was invalid because of an error or omission on the part of the Regional Returning Officers, Local Returning Officers or their respective staffs. There is no provision in RPA 1983 which deprives a Regional Returning Officer or Local Returning Officer of their charges in respect of a by-election which follows a successful election petition. Where an election petition, however, complains of the conduct of the Regional Returning Officer or Local Returning Officer and he/she is deemed respondent to that position, they would need to pay any legal costs incurred.

Both Regional Returning Officers and Local Returning Officers will wish to be satisfied that they are protected by adequate personal insurance cover, and that any relevant policies are not subject to unacceptable excess levels or conditions." (European Parliamentary Election Guidance 2004, written by the current author for the Electoral Commission)

The following is taken from similar guidance for the 2005 Westminster parliamentary election:

"If a parliamentary election has to be re-run, the Government may be prepared to offer a general indemnity to ensure that no-

*one is out of pocket. Such claims will only be considered if they
are reasonable, solely attributable to the election, and if all other
recourse is exhausted. The Government reserves the right to
refuse to offer an indemnity if the claim results from a failure to
follow advice and/or guidance given by either the then DCA or the
Electoral Commission."*

Although there is considerable comfort in the above words, there is an
equal lack of precision which is unsatisfactory for lawyers, particularly
in the insurance field. This is an area that must be developed and
clarified in the future – some type of formal indemnity drafted by a
specialist QC (as independent between Government and practitioners)
would be one way forward. Indeed, as is quoted elsewhere in this
book, some guidance from both the Electoral Commission and DCA is
general, ambivalent and open to interpretation.

In the meantime, traditional arguments recur over the policies at local
level. Some authorities, in the face of ever-diminishing resources, have
particularly astringent auditors or insurance officers who believe that
because the Returning Officer takes separate fees for election work
then the *quid pro quo* is that they should be used to finance his/her
insurance cover. This has been resisted by several senior Returning
Officers who, first of all, find it difficult to separate out of a large block
policy the exact size of this small premium which, in any event, is
included as standard in the Zurich Mutual policy. Again, counsel's
opinion has been sought (many years ago) that this is all incidental to
the general power to employ staff and the incumbent duty to appoint
a Returning Officer. Although not seemingly designed to cover the
point, it could be argued that the Local Authorities (Indemnities for
Members and Officers) Order of 2004 (S.I. No. 3082) deals with the
issue quite adequately.

There is also plenty of advice to keep adequate records of incidents that
might lead to insurance claims. Counsel also value contemporaneous

notes if litigation ensues after the poll. Such advice might be entirely reasonable in the calmness of a seminar room or the pages of an election guidance manual, but in the hustle and bustle of a busy election office it is often quite understandably overlooked.

Again, the Electoral Commission now produces advice on risk management, a topic which has grown in significance over recent years. Many authorities have some expert resource in this area and the Commission have produced a sample risk log. As they rightly point out, prevention is better than cure as, in many cases, electoral law does not provide for a remedy other than by way of election petition (and possible re-run of the election).

Fortunately, many Returning Officers and Electoral Administrators have no contact at all with insurance companies, but those that do when embroiled with the small print might agree with the quote from Peter Schaffer's play, *Sleuth*:

> *"...Insurance...Aah...now the plot thickens..."*

Chapter 12

POSTAL VOTING

"...post o'er Land and Ocean without rest..." Milton

This chapter has been deliberately entitled "Postal Voting" rather than "Absent Voting" (as including proxy voting) as postal voting is probably the most controversial and difficult topic, bar none, in modern electoral administration. What was, say over 10 years ago, a rather dreary and arcane practice that attracted very little interest is now labelled as "a charter for cheats" and "a fiddle". The turning point was really to allow postal voting on demand (2001) rather than only granting the facility to the infirm or those away on business (never really checked by electoral staff). A worthy idea to combat falling turnout – voting by post is more convenient for the elector in today's pressurised world – there was a huge expansion in demand for postal votes: 15% (almost 4 million) of total votes cast at the 2005 General Election compared with 2.4% in 1997. Real problems then began with a number of high profile cases of fraud and corruption within the system that made headlines in the national media, the most famous being the Birmingham case in 2005 ("...a system that would disgrace a banana republic", "the postal vote envelopes may as well have steal me printed on the front", "the Returning Officer threw the rule book out of the window", etc.). Unsurprisingly, a legislative reaction came from the Government with the introduction of security/personal identifiers for those exercising the franchise by post (first used in May 2007 in England and Wales).

All that this has achieved is the creation of an immensely cumbersome process that is awkward to negotiate for the voter (many of whom are elderly and struggle with bureaucratic paperwork) and, frighteningly, sometimes borders on the utterly impossible to administer for the

Returning Officer/Electoral Administrator. It is a classic example of tinkering with an old system (started after the Great War to allow the military to vote) and trying to make it work in the entirely different technological culture of the 21st Century. Like many parts of the electoral system, the case for reform after a period of research and considered reflection is overwhelming – but unlikely to occur in the near future. Although beyond the scope of this book, other democracies tackle the issue in different ways, e.g. nationals abroad voting at polling stations within their embassies.

Key issues

From a practical point of view, there are a number of key issues:

- Don't underestimate the task – it requires considerable attention.

- Do employ an adequate number of staff (and this is resource intensive over a short burst of time).

- Do expect lots of criticism if incorrect ballot packs are sent out or even correct ones dispatched a few days late.

- As a corollary, don't expect any praise if you achieve this on time.

- Don't believe everything will be all right and everyone will live happily ever after by relying heavily on outside contractors; high levels of personal involvement are required from election staff.

The Electoral Commission formulated a similar conclusion in their report on the May 2007 local elections in England:

"Managing postal votes is a substantial task in itself, even though in some authorities less than 10% of the electorate vote by post. Unless properly resourced and staffed, the management of the postal vote exercise, with the significant amount of staff time it involves, risks the diversion of resources from polling day and the count."

The question of the address

Considering the process itself (this text will avoid a lengthy procedural description for that is covered in other manuals), there are a number of rather awkward technical rules that can cause problems. For instance, when a postal vote is requested to be sent to an address that is different from the address at which the elector is registered, a reason for such redirection must be given, e.g. caring for a sick relative, holiday, etc. This seems quite straightforward but suppose the elector simply states "that's what I want" or "it's just better" or something similar. It is submitted that these are not explanations adequate enough to meet the test in the regulations to explain the circumstances so as to require delivery to a different address. If possible, this should be pursued with the applicant but, as ever, the Electoral Registration Officer is best advised to accept explanations on face value – it is not his or her role to investigate the nature of the temporary sojourn. However, there must be some explanation and it would seem entirely reasonable to look for some evidential base rather than a reason akin to personal whimsy.

If a large number of postal votes are being sent to one address (as referred to in the example described in the chapter on Electoral Integrity) then, at least, the Electoral Registration Officer should be suspicious and consider calling the police. Naturally, some addresses are entirely *bona fide* in this respect – HMOs, student residences, elderly persons care homes, etc. but some are certainly not. A London Borough made a serious error once at a parliamentary election in sending 200 postal votes to a disused factory when plainly no-one was resident. It is accepted that the pressure is high to complete the dispatch of postal vote packs as soon as possible, but serious errors like this have to be avoided. Many Electoral Registration Officers agree a threshold number for a single address with their local police "SPOC" and notify the constabulary if that number is reached. It is important that this number reflects local circumstances in that the number of students, for example, varies in different towns and cities.

Waivers

Another contentious point from 2007 was the use of the waiver provisions. Postal voting now works on the basis of two personal identifiers (signature and birthday) being provided to the Electoral Registration Officer prior to the election for retention within the records and, then, these are checked against a security statement containing the personal identifiers that accompanies the postal ballot. But what about those unable to provide a signature through disability or illiteracy? Those people should not be discriminated against and should be allowed to vote by post, often helped by a relative or friend. Thus, the regulations allow the Electoral Registration Officer to waive this requirement if satisfied on the grounds of disability or illiteracy. But what level of proof or evidence is required? How is this to be applied nationally to avoid local variations? Some Returning Officers in 2007 reported receiving several hundred waiver applications at a time and became very suspicious, especially when they were brought into their offices from only one or two sources. Shortly before the May 2007 local elections, the Electoral Commission helpfully drafted a sample waiver application but some highly awkward decisions had to be made in several election offices at very short notice and under the usual pressurised circumstances. The Electoral Commission advice is well meaning but surely platitudinous:

> *"Your policy for responding to requests for waivers should be robust to ensure the integrity of the voting system while allowing such electors access to the absent voting system" Guidance manual for May 2007 local elections*

In their subsequent report on the same elections, the Commission comment in a critical manner on Electoral Registration Officers whom they believe went too far (beyond their statutory powers?) in asking for additional non-statutory forms to be completed or attestations to be acquired when this was not required by statute. The use of these forms, they continue, was insensitive to electors who were requesting a waiver on the grounds of physical disability. The Commission also record the disappointment of many disability groups at the way in which waivers were handled by Electoral Registration Officers. To give some balance to the argument (and in modest defence of Electoral Registration Officers), it would be interesting to see what attitude would have been taken had such steps exposed fraudulent activity on, say, the Birmingham scale of 2004; or worse still, if it had only been discovered at a later stage, probably in the courts. Could the same report have contained criticism of Electoral Registration Officers for failing to check such waiver applications thoroughly? It is not easy being an Electoral Registration Officer/Returning Officer and well nigh impossible to win all the time...

Collecting the identifiers at the start of 2007 also created a considerable burden of work and new problems. Many absent voters (probably about a third) required a reminder to submit the identifiers, some provided three sample signatures ("just to be on the safe side"), some refused as this was the Big Brother state collecting more personal records intruding upon their freedom and, as a real highlight, some people submitted their birthday as "after the May election date"! The regulations do not contain a discretion and although some queries can be pursued, unless valid identifiers are recorded, no postal vote will be issued.

As ever, the parties continue their canvassing among their supporters and submit postal (and proxy) vote applications on their behalf. Unfortunately, in 2007, some Electoral Registration Officers were rejecting these as they did not match their own forms from their suppliers that could be processed electronically. This is incorrect – the Electoral Registration Officer must accept any application that contains the required information and arrives before the deadline.

Problems with the process

The real issue with postal vote administration (dispatch and receipt) is that it is a laborious, tedious, resource hungry, lengthy process. Most authorities had an opening of postal votes every day for 10 days or so before polling day on 3rd May 2007. Some of these lasted most of the working day. Interestingly, many reported a distinct lack of interest from candidates and agents in the process, after an initial brief phase of attendance; watching security statements being passed through a scanner is not too exciting! Certain stages have been rightly mechanised but horrible problems arose in 2007 with the software at many authorities. Either it did not work at all when it eventually arrived or was distinctly random and temperamental in its checking of identifiers. Up against a tough timetable, some simply abandoned the technology and reverted to manual checking. The AEA report on those local elections contains some appalling experiences at authorities throughout the country, with staff having to work long hours under great stress.

The regulations state that at least 20% of returned postal votes have to be checked for signature/birthday accuracy. As events unfolded in 2007, this turned out to be a useful safety valve for, in a number of authorities, good intentions to check 100% had to be abandoned due to software failure. Total statistical returns from all authorities were not yet available at the time of writing but it is probable that two-thirds of all wards (constituencies in Wales) were 100% checked. About 10% received the minimum 20% check. The English Metropolitan Districts were the best performers, carrying out a 100% check on postal votes in over 82% of all wards.

It was thought by many Returning Officers and Electoral Administrators in 2007 that actually checking the signatures for the first time would be a forensic nightmare. Expertise in this area was (and still is) pretty limited in local government. A circular was sent out by the Electoral Commission describing "the shape, pen-path and fluency" of signature recognition but, as that was only received after 12th April, there was very little time to become expert in this new science. Nevertheless, this process of checking proved to be a lot more straightforward than many had anticipated. A robust commonsense view was taken by virtually all to only disallow signatures if they could not, under reasonable viewing, be said to resemble the signature held on record.

The position was well explained in the Electoral Commission Circular referred to above and should be followed in future:

> *"....err on the side of inclusion and only reject postal voting statements when fully satisfied that the signature provided on the statement is not that provided at application. The Returning Officer should be confident that a signature shows major and significant differences to the control signature before deciding they are not satisfied. In summary, unless the Returning Officer can be certain that the signature is unsatisfactory the signature should be accepted."*

Obviously, the position with dates of birth could allow no flexibility and even some pre-printed forms with DD/MM/19.. were replaced with the date of signing. Again, some people are not used to using 03-06, etc. and, as an afterthought, inserted a zero after the day, causing their vote to be disallowed. There are some entirely unconfirmed stories of one or two experienced Electoral Administrators sympathetic to the confusion of elderly voters choosing to put some of these statements and ballots into the unchecked pile (as checking less than 100%) so that they could be allowed through...

Despite the need to collect these identifiers there was not a significant decline in the number of postal votes issued in 2007. In 2006, some had felt that demand had clearly peaked for this type of voting; people were being deterred by the fraud scare reports in the national media and, in any event, there cannot be an infinite demand for postal votes in the system. The following table shows the figures for 2007 as compared to earlier years.

Postal ballot papers issued as % of electorate

	2007	(General Election – 2005)
Wales	12.5%	12.7%
	2006	
English Districts	11.9%	13.1%
English Unitaries	13.1%	13.6%
English Metropolitans	15.07%	13.1%

It is interesting to note the increase in the Metropolitan Districts; certain towns had a huge increase, presumably the result of vigorous political party activity.

Were more postal ballots rejected under this system than the previous witnessed declaration of identity process? The number rejected as a percentage of the number returned was 3.2% in England in 2007 compared with an average of 3.02% in the 2006 local elections and 2.47% at the General Election in 2005. In Wales, 6.2% were rejected, exactly the same figure as in 2003. At the General Election in 2005, 4.6% of returned postal ballots were rejected in Wales. Thus, despite some of the scare stories in the media, the position overall looks not to have changed unfavourably to any great extent.

Why were postal votes rejected? The following Electoral Commission table is based on responses from nearly 200 English authorities.

Reasons for postal vote rejection in England

Rejected for	% of rejected postal votes
Want of signature	18.8
Want of date of birth	10.7
Want of both	12.8
Mismatched signature	26.6
Mismatched date of birth	22.4
Both mismatched	8.6

(In Wales the biggest single cause of rejection was failure to match dates of birth, not signature.)

Whatever the ups and downs of these figures, the problems associated with checking postal votes are not going to disappear. Postal voting is clearly here to stay and the figures show it is not declining rapidly in popularity. Moreover, the Electoral Commission believe strongly that 100% checking should be mandatory after the 2008 elections and before the next UK parliamentary election. Before such a parliamentary election is held, it will be essential to resolve (if possible) the dreadful software problems encountered by authorities in 2007. The situation will only become more acute at such an election, for there are a good number of constituencies that cross local authority boundaries; Wales experienced problems in this respect in 2007 as disks of data supplied by one Council to another could not, in some cases, be read and some Electoral Registration Officers had to resort to supplying records in paper copies.

This particular issue arose again in the Sedgefield parliamentary by-election of 2007; that constituency included three District Councils, only two of which used the same software. This was the software that records and stores the absent voter lists and their personal identifiers collected by the Electoral Registration Officer of each authority. Arrangements had to be made to supply these lists and identifiers to the Acting Returning Officer to facilitate the checking of postal ballots. For this by-election, the Acting Returning Officer decided to keep the data in three separate electronic files and to print postal voting statements in three different colours, one for each Council area. In this way, they could be easily identified, collated and scanned against the correct record. The Acting Returning Officer at Sedgefield stated that this system worked well; over 70% of 13,637 postal votes were received back for checking and less than 1% were rejected.

Although this is all highly admirable, much was achieved because of the excellent co-operation between the authorities, which might not be replicated throughout the country in a UK Parliamentary General Election. Remember also that Sedgefield were relying heavily on electronic data for they had no access to paper records other than their own. It was, apparently, not an issue at this by-election but, again, in a UK-wide General Election, different experiences could easily prevail.

This is hardly satisfactory and the Electoral Commission believes the way forward is for the Government to establish a central mechanism for Great Britain-wide storage, maintenance and exchange of absent voter identifier records. They believe that most of this work can be undertaken by the software suppliers but the practical experiences and results from 2006/07 cannot fill anyone with confidence. Much hard work, training and learning has still to be done generally with regard to postal voting.

Chapter 13

FINANCE

"Wine maketh merry: but money answereth all things"
Ecclesiastes 10 (19)

Elections and money are not particularly close companions and, indeed, at many points their relationship is a strained one. Whether it be the constant complaint that parliamentary elections are under-funded from the centre (and hence heavily subsidised by local authorities) or that staff are poorly paid (and do not want to carry out polling day duties), the cry here is that in the UK we have "democracy on the cheap". The last General Election cost over £70 million and, in large authorities, election budgets will be in the region of seven figures (registration included). Thus, by any standards, substantial sums are involved – however, most who work in the electoral world say they do the job to benefit our democracy and certainly not for the money!

The starting point is that the source of the election pays for the cost of running the election. Local authorities pay for their own elections and Whitehall funds parliamentary elections (including European). Some District Councils do not send Parish Councils bills for their elections, though most do charge. National referendums are funded centrally (the last being the 1975 Common Market issue) but those for directly elected mayors will be met from local resources. In two-tier areas, Boroughs and Districts virtually always undertake the running of the County Council elections and are re-imbursed their costs, though not, it may be said, without some disputation in recent years. This is not surprising as local authority budgets are now under very considerable pressure and, moreover, many years ago, in some areas, the county elections were carried out "free of charge" at District level in return for the County Council administering the staff superannuation fund. It is believed that practices of this sort have now ceased.

Accounts

Separate accounts are required for all election work and it is quite common for Returning Officers to have several bank accounts in their name for different types of elections. Indeed, for European elections separate accounts were operated in the Eastern Region for both Regional Returning Officer and Local Returning Officer, even though technically the same person. The accounts are usually styled with the Returning Officer's name plus a description of the election. They need not all be at the same bank or even at the bank the local authority uses, but a proliferation of accounts at several banks is harder to manage. At a practical level, the situation often looks messy and there is no simple tidy answer. Local circumstances often have developed over a period of time to produce a workable (or not?) situation.

Like all other matters electoral, the responsibility, at the end of the day, rests with the Returning Officer for these accounts and payments therefrom. Of course, the usual practice is to have a number of authorised signatures and the Returning Officer may not now be required to sign any cheques (still in considerable use, even though BACs payments are more common). Whatever financial arrangements are in place, they need to be clear, accountable and, above all, able to move along at a reasonable pace. To receive payment for election duties in the August after a May poll is slow by any standards and hardly likely to encourage staff in either their current work or to re-apply for future election duties. Prompt payment should be aimed for, though the practice of paying staff on the day in cash by touring round polling stations could not be recommended. Twenty or so years ago this did occur but it would be considered both unsafe and impractical today.

Scales of fees and charges

All elections should have a fixed fees and charges scale. Although the point may seem obvious, it is both surprising and uncomfortable to learn that many Returning Officers do not know this and have never seen the fee scale until after the election when they receive, or do not receive, payments (for some authorities "include" local election fees in the Chief Executive salary). For local elections, the authority fixes the scale of fees and charges (increased by an inflation index every year), usually in liaison with neighbouring authorities (county-wide) so as to have consistency in payment and stop the "poaching" of staff from other Councils. This is sometimes a tricky issue for a number of shire Districts, for instance, when their boundaries adjoin Metropolitan Districts. In the West Midlands, for example, a number of staff employed in the large cities lived in the surrounding counties and preferred to work in polling stations at their domiciled market town or village. Similar considerations apply to London, with many staff commuting in from the Home Counties. This is addressed in the fee scales so that there is both an inner and outer London weighting to encourage staff to work in the conurbation, often staying overnight on the Wednesday in a hotel to facilitate the early start on polling Thursday. Indeed, some of the adjoining Councils say that their staff are attracted by this extra weighting and therefore work in London rather than for their home authority. Moreover, some of the more distant Home Counties authorities claim the same problem and ask for the "roseland" weighting to be extended for parliamentary electors. This has always been resisted by Government officials who, to be fair to them, have to draw a line somewhere, with unhappiness an inevitable consequence for those on the wrong side of the fence. People commute from far afield into London with speedy inter-city trains (Yorkshire, South Wales, etc.) so it is impossible to have an ideal solution, but none of this makes staff recruitment any easier (especially for experienced staff).

Fees and Charges Orders for parliamentary elections are not easy documents to read and, like much of our electoral system, overdue for reform. The Electoral Administration Act of 2006 contains Section 68 which appears to give more flexibility to reimburse Returning Officers for all their necessary services at a parliamentary election up to a fixed amount and authorise, in certain situations, extra payments – e.g. security? It is to be hoped that prior to the next General Election, guidance will be published as to how Ministry of Justice officials envisage this operating in practice.

Dealing with the Electoral Claims Unit

The current guidance dates from the 2005 General Election and emanates from the Electoral Claims Unit based at Hemel Hempstead. It runs to some 40 pages and starts by pointing out there have been instances where expenditure on various items has been judged by the Electoral Claims Unit to be neither reasonable nor necessary; claims must be submitted within 12 months and "good luck with the completion of the claim form"! What areas of claim are rejected as unreasonable/unnecessary? The following is a sample from the extensive list:

- Lighting outside polling stations and count centres.

- First Aid kits.

- Floral decorations at count centres.

- Refreshments for non-counting personnel at the count (i.e. to exclude police, security staff, etc.), though claims for light refreshments for staff will be reimbursed.

- Loss of revenues at places where the count is held, e.g. loss of bar takings at leisure centres.

Experiences between local authority electoral staff and the Electoral Claims Unit are of a mixed quality, though probably better in the current climate than in earlier years. There are accurate – but happily very old – stories such as that of a Returning Officer living in retirement receiving very threatening letters from the Electoral Claims Unit saying that he had made (and been paid) a false claim for flowers on the stage at the count. Unless the sum was reimbursed promptly then proceedings in court would ensue. The retired Returning Officer (who had ceased being Chief Executive/Returning Officer a couple of years earlier) did send back a cheque for less than £10 to remedy this heinous misdemeanour and heard nothing more...

Seeking recompense for bar takings at a high profile count where security closed the venue a week earlier has been a similarly futile task, albeit involving larger sums of money. Despite the personal protestations from the Chief Executive/Returning Officer (experienced in such matters as the barrelage of public houses because of planning inquiries/housing clearance areas in the North of England), this was considered as totally non-refundable. Indeed, it would be fair to say that the then Electoral Claims Unit (and Home Office in those days) could not grasp at all how takings could be accurately quantified for licensed premises. Whilst such care with public funds may be commendable on its face, it is simply recorded as a loss to the local authority's accounts. Worse still, there are entirely unconfirmed and totally unsupportable stories of some "creativity" in the completion of the claim form to attempt to redress such perceived unfairness at local level; for example, heating costs at a large counting hall during a warm summer evening/day were considerable, yet approved without question by the Electoral Claims Unit.

For parliamentary elections, the Electoral Claims Unit advance to all Regional Returning Officers 75% of the amount they spent at the last general election. This usually appears in reasonable time after the writ is issued and it is possible to claim for up to 90% if you can convince the Electoral Claims Unit with a plausible explanation. In 2005 there were special worries in Whitehall about electoral fraud (aftermath of Birmingham case, etc.) and extra funds could be made available for any special measures, if agreed with the Electoral Claims Unit in advance. Interest earned on advances made has to be accounted for back to the Electoral Claims Unit and it may not be used to offset expenditure elsewhere.

Grants are also available to purchase essential equipment to run a parliamentary election, at either 80% or 50% of the cost. The 80% applies to essential items such as polling screens, ballot boxes, etc. The 50% applies to so-called "discretionary" items such as temporary ramps for polling stations, counting tables and computer software packages. They are termed discretionary (according to the Electoral Claims Unit) because they assist both financially and administratively but are not absolutely essential. Moreover, these items may be used for other election purposes, it is claimed.

Such views are not uncontested by those who administer elections but that is the practice followed. Again, for most of these grants to be forthcoming the old-fashioned practice of obtaining three competitive quotes must be observed and, for software, evidence should be produced that the product is self-financing – that means clear net savings to the Exchequer over a ten-year period. It is said that the Electoral Claims Unit can sometimes be reasonably flexible over the details of such requirements but, in the context of modern procurement practice in the public sector, their guide has a negative approach and it is hoped that improvements can be made in the future following the 2006 Act.

On a more positive note, the (then) DCA did recognise the problems that local authorities were encountering over the new postal vote security provisions (2006/07) and did make extra funding available. Interestingly, this was ring-fenced to the collection of those identifiers and their checking via new software. The funds were not huge – tens of thousands of pounds for most councils – and, as usual, the remaining costs of scanners and software licences had to be funded from existing IT budgets.

Local authority budgets

The big picture here is one of local authorities not being properly funded for election work. Central Government Departments make bold claims that tens of millions are paid to Councils but the Revenue Support Grant system (highly arcane and archaic) then masks actual payment into the authority's general funds. The system of "floors and ceilings" means that, from year to year, the Revenue Support Grant should not fluctuate wildly but it can prevent new payments getting into the system as intended. This has been taken up with Ministers at the Ministry of Justice and the Department for Communities and Local Government but reforming local government finance is a task of Herculean size that requires more than the wisdom of Solomon (remember the Layfield and Lyons reports?). To be obliged to do this to accommodate alleged shortfalls in election payments is simply unthinkable in Whitehall. Ring-fencing some of this money out of the RSG has been talked about and keenly supported by the AEA. However, the current policy of the Local Government Association has been to oppose more special grants as reducing the ability of local authorities to make decisions at local levels about their spending. Inevitably, the ring-fenced money would not be new or extra so local government sees this as a negative, particularly as Central Government is vigorous with capping any Council Tax rises above 5% at present. It all means less flexibility and less room to manoeuvre for Councils.

The elections finance question has been caught up with all this and there are estimates that parliamentary elections are subsidised by about 20 to 30% from local authority coffers. The problems of finance were looked at by the Electoral Commission some years ago (2001/02 – report published) but there appears to be little likelihood of substantial change in the near future – the Comprehensive Spending Review of Autumn 2007 setting out public expenditure plans for the next three years is a tough settlement (effectively only 1% growth).

At local level, the picture is not too much more encouraging. At one authority, members are actively considering moving to elections once every four years rather than the thirds they operate at present. And the reason why? Simply to save money. In a way, it is sad to record such thinking, for it ignores key issues such as encouraging democratic participation, but it does show the pressure on local authority budgets.

And, so, do you have to be an accountant to be a successful Returning Officer? Many Chief Executives are so qualified but about the same number are lawyers. Is it an advantage to have a financial background to tackle these issues? The answer to both questions is a pretty clear "No", for election finance is not excessively/intricately complex when compared with other aspects of local government accounting. Most of the accounts discussed in this chapter are usually handled perfectly competently by election officers who do not have CIPFA/ACA qualifications. Some authorities have imported a qualified accountant to deal with account preparation but this is not too common. What is more common is a struggle after a parliamentary election to submit accounts to the Electoral Claims Unit on time because invoices from outside sources have not been tendered satisfactorily or there is some similar delay. There are stories that circulate in the electoral world of local authorities not having their General Election accounts approved before the next General Election came around in 4/5 years' time… Government Departments responsible for elections talk about appalling delays, publishing name and shame lists, stopping Acting Returning Officer's fees, etc. In return, some senior Returning Officers have talked about having an amnesty, persuading the Electoral Claims Unit to accept accounts as "near enough for Government work", occasionally on the basis that the person who had prepared them has not only left the employment of the authority but is now dead!

There are a vast amount of small technical issues that are regular queries in this area and practice does vary from authority to authority. Thus, should higher rate tax-payers have 40% deducted directly from their election payments rather than the standard 22%? Most authorities probably follow the latter course simply for consistency and ease of administration, leaving those few to make appropriate personal self-assessment returns. However, 40% deduction is not unknown and is referred to in Electoral Commission guidance. What is important is to make the tax deduction (National Insurance is not payable on staff fees) and account to HM Revenue and Customs accordingly. Some staff – usually those retired or unemployed – are exempt and have to so certify to the Returning Officer's staff. Generally, this works quite well but in several hundred there are always one or two who forget and try to reclaim tax deducted – extra work that is really not welcome.

An audit of election accounts?

Should election accounts (particularly for local elections) be subject to the Council's overall audit programme? Strictly speaking they are not part of the Council's overall accounts as they are in the name of the Returning Officer and, therefore, separate. Very many years ago, the old Town Clerks would use their existing private accounts, receive monies as advanced by their employing authorities and pay out only by their personal cheques. Such practices have now ceased but some authorities still contain some personal rivalries/differences between Chief Executive and Director of Finance. Again, practice varies but the traditional custom was for the Returning Officer (not acting as Chief Executive) to invite the internal auditors to "look over" the election accounts – after all, it is the Council's money being used here. This is still resisted, at some authorities, mainly as a result of historical tension. Sometimes, horror stories appear: at an authority in South Wales a couple of years ago, downright criminal activity was eventually exposed in that electoral staff were making personal withdrawals of hugely excessive amounts unbeknown to all, including the Returning Officer. Criminal cases followed in the courts with successful prosecutions.

Combined elections accounts

Combined elections (see Chapter 15) bring another dimension to the finance question but no great joy! In 2005, the Electoral Commission advised that:

> *"Preparing election accounts for combined elections can be extremely complex and time-consuming."*

The basic idea is that costs are split 50/50 between the two polls, local/ parliamentary or by thirds when there are three. Of course that only applies in areas subject to combination – for example, some County divisions may not be contested – and only to costs which are not solely attributable to one election. Mathematically, this can get convoluted. Thus, for the general clerical fund there is an extra 15% authorised for a combined poll. This is reclaimed pro rata, so that if there are 10 divisions of which 5 are combined, then the 15% figure is divided by 10 and the result multiplied by 5. With this sort of complication, it is quite understandable that there are delays in submitting accounts to the Electoral Claims Unit after combined polls and, moreover, the same unit often raise a good number of queries on the documents submitted.

Hopefully some progress can be made to reform such a testing process. An idea submitted by senior Returning Officers many years ago to the Home Office was to give each parliamentary constituency a set allowance of about £80/90,000 (at 2006/07) and then give the Acting Returning Officer broad discretion as to its allocation. In return for this discretion, accounts would be kept to show spending, etc. but not necessarily in the Electoral Claims Unit format with all their involved sub-headings. The broader discretionary approach continues to be pressed by SOLACE but, it must be said, without any particular success at the time of writing. The ideal solution would be for this to be implemented alongside "a robust, publicly available electoral modernisation strategy" which the Electoral Commission again called for in August 2007. It is important that the topic of finance does not become entirely separated from electoral modernisation, for the two concepts are inextricably linked. Those in the electoral world will watch for the Government response with interest, though as always with both patience and, sadly, sometimes with resignation.

Chapter 14

THE ELECTION TIMETABLE

"We haven't the time to take our time" Eugene Ionesco

"We must use time as a tool not as a couch"
John F Kennedy

The electoral timetable is something of an enigma to those charged with running elections. On one hand it has some clear deadlines whereby a particular task must be achieved or some particular activity ceases. This can be most useful, for it enables the Returning Officer to say that a nomination will not be accepted after the deadline or a postal vote application will not be processed for it has been received too late. These are absolute rules and there is no discretion to extend these deadlines – indeed, the widely held view of most lawyers is that they could not be properly extended by the courts, even in the already cited example of a postal strike delaying receipt of postal votes. There is no doubt that Parliament has firmly fixed the timetable in legislation.

However, on the other hand, the timetable as currently drafted is highly demanding (and unforgiving) in the context of running elections in the 21st Century. It has its original roots in the more sedate world of Victorian Britain, when there was time to deal with fewer nominations and post notices on the village notice board. It has been modified over the years but concentrates a highly complex administrative process into a few weeks. It might not recognise weekends in its time calculations but, without fear of contradiction, most Electoral Administrators will be busy working over Saturdays and Sundays to carry out all the necessary processes. And this is the real rub. However much you try, it is simply not going to be possible to invent/manufacture time and whilst extra resources can be sought, extra days cannot. Hence the need to project plan, prepare thoroughly and tackle as many work issues as reasonably practicable before the actual timetable starts running from the Notice of Election. The situation is always compounded in its arduousness by the many factors outside the direct control of election staff, as recent elections have graphically indicated: late/non delivery of software, failure by printers, problems with Royal Mail deliveries.

Many new to the administration of elections often ask when is the best time to start preparation? Those with experience usually answer at the end of the previous election, holding a post-mortem into those arrangements! For those authorities operating elections by thirds, this is particularly true as many in their "fallow" year may now have a County Council election, combined with a General Election. With the European election and, probably, parish and town elections, these authorities never really have a year off to, for instance, change their software supplier. This is a process best carried out over a period of months, not weeks, as it is never a good idea to go live in an actual electoral situation with brand new software but it is always wise to have a thorough test period, as events over recent years have shown. For those with all-out elections every four years, the electoral cycle is a little more generous, but staff at these authorities might argue otherwise! Indeed, they often maintain their work is harder as they (and associated systems/staff) are sometimes a little out of peak condition when election time comes around.

Another significant issue with the timetable is that it is subtly different for every election, which sometimes can create confusion. Moreover, when there is a combined election, one timetable must take precedence: usually the parliamentary one. All this simply adds to any confusion rather than clarifying the position – different agents and candidates for different elections within one timetable can easily get mixed up over deadlines.

Turning now to consider the details of some timetables, a local government (2007) and parliamentary (2005) timetable are set out below.

LOCAL GOVERNMENT 2007 ELECTION TIMETABLE

Proceeding	Day
Deadline for application to be included on the register of electors to be used for nomination	Wednesday 7th February
Notice of election to be published	Not later than Tuesday 27th March
Delivery of nomination papers	During office hours on any day from the date of publication of the Notice of Election
Last day for delivery of nomination papers	Not later than noon on Wednesday 4th April
Publish statement as to persons nominated	Not later than noon on Tuesday 10th April
Last day for withdrawals of candidature	Not later than noon on Wednesday 11th April
Last day for notice of appointment of election agents	Not later than noon on Wednesday 11th April
Deadline for applications to be included on the register of electors to be used at the election	Wednesday 18th April
Last day for requests for a new postal vote or to change or cancel an existing postal vote or proxy appointment	Not later than 5.00pm on Wednesday 18th April
Issue of postal ballot papers	Not earlier than 5.00pm on Wednesday 18th April
Publish notice of poll	Not later than Wednesday 25th April
Last date for new applications to vote by proxy (except for medical emergencies)	Not later than 5.00pm on Wednesday 25th April
Last day for notice of appointment of counting agents and polling agents	Not later than Thursday 26th April

First day to issue ballot papers in response to requests to replace lost postal ballot papers	Friday 27th April
Polling Day	Thursday 3rd May (7.00am to 10.00pm)
Last day to issue replacements for spoilt or lost postal ballot papers	Not later than 5.00pm on Thursday 3rd May
Last for new applications to vote by proxy on grounds of medical emergency	Not later than 5.00pm on Thursday 3rd May
Last day to make alterations to the register to correct a clerical error or to implement a court (registration appeal) decision	Not later than 9.00pm on Thursday 3rd May
Last day for the receipt of return of election expenses if declaration of the result is before midnight on polling day	Thursday 7th June
Last day for the receipt of return of election expenses if declaration of the result is after midnight on polling day but before the next day	Friday 8th June

UK PARLIAMENTARY GENERAL ELECTION TIMETABLE 2005

Proceeding	Day
Dissolution of old parliament/ issue of writ	Monday 11th April
Receipt of the writ	Tuesday 12th April
Notice of election: to be published not later than 4.00pm on	Thursday 14th April
Delivery of nomination papers: between the hours of 10.00am and 4.00pm on any day after the date of publication of the notice of election	Friday 15th April
Last day of delivery of nomination papers: not later than 4.00pm on	Tuesday 19th April
Last day for withdrawals of candidature: not later than 4.00pm on	Tuesday 19th April
Last day for notice of appointment of election agents: not later than 4.00pm on	Tuesday 19th April
Making of objections to nomination papers: between 10.00am to 4.00pm (or exceptionally between 10.00am and 5.00pm) on	Tuesday 19th April
Publish statement as to persons nominated (including notice of poll) and list of polling stations: 5.00pm on	Tuesday 19th April
Last day for requests to change or cancel existing postal vote or proxy appointment: not later than 5.00pm on	Tuesday 19th April
Last day for new applications to vote by post or proxy: not later than 5.00pm on	Tuesday 26th April

Last day to make alterations to the register of electors to correct a clerical error or to implement a court (registration appeal) decision	Wednesday 27th April
First day to issue ballot papers in response to requests to replace lost postal ballot papers (England and Wales)	Thursday 28th April
First day to issue ballot papers in response to requests to replace lost postal ballot papers (Scotland)	Friday 29th April
Last day of notice of appointment of counting agents and polling agents	Tuesday 3rd May
Last day to issue replacement spoilt or lost postal ballot papers: not later than 5.00pm on	Wednesday 4th May
Polling day (7.00am to 10.00pm)	Thursday 5th May
Last day for the receipt of return of election expenses – within 35 days after the day on which the result of the election is declared (assuming declaration of the result after midnight on polling day)	Friday 10th June

Certain key dates and deadlines are clearly shown, but if no specific time is stated then the deadline will be 12 midnight on that day (but there is no requirement for the Returning Officer/Electoral Administrator to be present then!). The second point worth noting is that for delivery of nomination papers the local timetable uses the well-worn cliché "office hours", presumably interpreted as 9.00am–5.00pm. The parliamentary timetable, however, states that delivery of nomination papers should be between 10.00am and 4.00pm until the deadline. (The rather quaint reason given for the lack of stipulated hours in the former instance is that the Returning Officer is not required to attend for delivery of papers.) Whatever the niceties of all this, electoral staff will probably be checking papers outside these hours, especially if there are hundreds of candidates for Parish Councils.

Time recording problems

It would be thought that the actual times in both timetables could not give rise to problems as we do not have different time zones in this country, unlike America or Russia. As ever with elections, this is not the case! So, it has been known for papers (relating to various parts of the process) to be received by fax at a local authority with a time recorded pre-dating the cut-off time. Should these be accepted if they are only picked up by election staff after the deadline? If the circumstances are such as to support receipt within the timescale then they should be, but what about the situation where paperwork is only collected after the deadline with a recorded time sent similarly outside the receipt period? Clearly, these should not be accepted but, in one case, the agent when challenged said it was because the automatic clock on the fax machine at his office had not been altered to the correct time (the clocks had changed the previous weekend) and, in fact, the paperwork (application for a postal vote) had been dispatched (only just) within time. What is the Returning Officer to do? The agent said that the clock had now been reset and it would never happen again..., etc. In that particular instance, the Returning Officer rejected the application following the usual line of looking at the paperwork on its face and making a decision, despite the unhappiness of the agent.

Some actions within the electoral timescale appear to have no deadline. The Electoral Commission cite the example of a candidate advising the Returning Officer of his/her guests that are intended to be invited to the count. The Electoral Commission maintain there is no formal statutory deadline for this but, in practice, for security reasons, there has to be some earlier notification. Most Returning Officers issue

133

admission tickets for their counts and keep a list of those attending. In very high profile counts, this list is run through a security service check well before polling day. All these very sensible precautions would be made meaningless if some people were allowed access to the count without proper screening. Fortunately, most agents and candidates accept such provisions as necessary and so do co-operate. However, this is not always the case: some Returning Officers have had calls from candidates (usually the weekend before polling day) with some plaintive pleas about their daughter's boyfriend who is travelling from afar to be at the count and it is his life's ambition to be present, etc., etc. Once such requests are granted, it is amazing to see them replicate themselves and become even more unreasonably late. If there is a public gallery, these people should be directed to it.

Dies non

In calculating the period of time for any elections, certain days are disregarded – traditionally described as *dies non*. These days are Saturdays, Sundays, Christmas Day, Good Friday, bank holidays and days appointed for public thanksgiving or mourning. Maundy Thursday was a casualty of the 2006 Electoral Administration Act and is now regarded as an ordinary working day; local authorities were already working on that day in any event.

Days designated as bank holidays come from the Banking and Finance Acts; thus, New Year's Day is a bank holiday in this respect. There are some regional variations too, e.g. St Patrick's Day in Northern Ireland (17th March, or 18th March if St Patrick's Day falls on a Sunday). This can produce complex variations in the electoral timetable, especially for by-elections. Thus in Northern Ireland and Scotland, at a General Election, 17th March and the first Monday in August would not be counted as they are bank holidays. But at a parliamentary by-election in England, they would be included as they are not bank holidays in this part of the United Kingdom.

National days of mourning and thanksgiving are rare, usually connected with events in the Royal Family but, as ever, should not be entirely dismissed for they could occur in the future.

The timetable spreads its tentacles...

Remember that the timetable applies to places outside the Electoral Administrator's office in the Town Hall – for example, at polling stations where all polling hours have now been standardised from 7.00am to 10.00pm (except parish polls which are still from 4.00pm to 9.00pm). Many administrators still report that the extra hour at the start and end of the day makes little difference to overall turnout and is usually pretty quiet. However, that is not to say that problems do not arise associated with these hours. All polling staff are lectured continuously on the importance of opening and closing on time, even if the premises may still be locked at 7.00am and the keyholder cannot be found. So polling has started, for instance, from the boot of the Presiding Officer's car or from the cycle sheds at the side of the school gate; but, at least, it has started on time. This is important as allegations of voters being denied access to the franchise are, at very best, embarrassing for the Returning Officer and, at worst, tricky to defend in subsequent petition proceedings. There is usually at least one polling station where an anxious voter has to catch a bus or train at or just before 7.00am to get to work, the hospital, grandma's funeral, etc. and wants to vote earlier than the official opening time. Regrettably, they must be (politely) refused for the polling stations open at 7.00am, not before and not later.

More commonly, there are voters who manage to leave their attendance at the polling station to the very last minute and rush in at 9.59pm or even later. At some busy stations, a queue can sometimes form around this time. What should the Presiding Officer do with people standing in the station waiting for their ballot papers? This is an issue where common practice and the exact technical legal position differ somewhat. The usual practice followed by many is to lock the doors of the station at 10.00pm but allow those voters who have entered to remain and vote, i.e. issue them with a ballot paper after the close of poll. This convention is not in accordance with the strict legal position which is that the voter must have been issued with a ballot paper before the 10.00pm close of poll. This is based on some reasonably old case law and several senior Returning Officers believe the principle could be challenged in the modern courts but, be that as it may, it is still the technically correct position.

The timetable sometimes has an effect on the fee scale for electoral staff. Thus, at the count, some authorities in the East used to have a fee scale devised to cover three hours' work or until after midnight (from the days when local polls used to close at 9.00pm, not at 10.00pm as now). A fixed fee was set and this increased by an hourly amount of every hour (or part thereof) after midnight. It is worth recording that several Returning Officers (well aware of the difficulties of counting staff recruitment) felt the need to recheck the results of a particular count at 11.55pm and move the actual announcement to "just after midnight!".

Timetable changes?

The foregoing clearly demonstrates that the electoral timetable is challenging for the Returning Officer/Electoral Administrator. The Electoral Commission have long recommended (since their 2005 report on the topic) that the timetable for UK parliamentary elections should be standardised at 25 working days – the same as for all other fixed-term elections. It is clearly not in the interests of electors (or administrators) to received poll cards late, or have their opportunity to register to vote (or to request a postal or proxy vote) limited by short timescales. In their by-election reports of 2006 and 2007, the Commission reiterated this view and recorded an apparent initial positive response from the Government. However, recent enquiries made by the author of the Ministry of Justice do indicate an issue or two to be resolved before such changes can be implemented. First, there is the not inconsiderable need for some primary legislation and parliamentary time is already oversubscribed by the current legislative programme. Secondly, there is a view amongst the mainstream political parties that to extend the electoral timetable simply increases the campaign costs; major parties probably spend in excess of a £1 million a day in the run-up to a Westminster poll, so to extend the timescale by more than a week or so would result in a huge increase in expenditure. The debts of the major parties are well documented in our media and there is considerable pressure on them to reduce campaign expenditure. Thus, what might appear a helpful suggestion to the Electoral Administrator may not be so appealing to the politicians.

Chapter 15

COMBINED ELECTIONS

"...when troubles come, they come not as single spies..."
William Shakespeare

Although never regarded as a complete novelty, combination of polls (to use the correct technical wording) has become much more common over recent years. The most common combination used to be districts and parishes, but parliamentary elections (both European and Westminster) are now increasingly being held on the same days as local elections. It has been suggested that this is to counteract voter fatigue but it is also probably closely connected with canvasser fatigue too. All the major parties have seen their membership slip compared to earlier years; there is simply a limit on the amount of leaflet distribution, house canvassing, poster fixing, etc. that people can achieve. To ask them to repeat all their work of May in the following June is to stretch resources considerably and people are reluctant to volunteer in the midst of already busy lives. Hence combination is more popular, particularly as many people vote solely on party lines – many residents when surveyed could not name their local councillor no matter how many years they may have served on the council.

Views amongst Returning Officers and Electoral Administrators vary on the stresses and strains of combination. The work virtually doubles and staff are deterred from working on even lengthier counts, especially if traditionally running into the early hours of the next day. Combined postal vote issues can be very demanding and ballot boxes appear to proliferate with no control! However, there is another view which is that it is the least worst option and does at least deal with the entire election process at one time; the disruptive element of election work is, at least, contained within a single time slot rather than being spread out over a longer time. There is a highly concentrated burst of activity but, at least, staff can return to normal duties after the count. The disruption to the school timetable is also diminished (a popular move) and there is a significant element of cost sharing (see Chapter 13 which deals with Finance). Some election staff say it is still not worth it despite the apparent advantages – views vary across the country.

There are a variety of complex statutory rules as to which polls *may* be combined and which *must* be combined; they cover both scheduled elections and by-elections. The best known postponement (i.e. the poll may not be combined) is that of Parish Councils not being held on the same day as a UK Parliamentary General Election. They are postponed for three weeks and this includes the scheduled elections and also elections to fill casual vacancies on that day. If that timetable has commenced and then a General Election is called, what happens to any nominations that would have been valid for the original date? The Electoral Commission's view is that these papers remain valid for the new poll; there is no provision for the Returning Officer to reject nomination papers on the grounds of postponement. In practical terms, postponements tend to diminish interest and turnout in parish elections – candidates complain about a sense of anti-climax and electors sometimes express puzzlement at having to vote so soon again. However, when postponed, the costs of running the parish (or community councils in Wales) elections are paid for out of the Consolidated Fund: claims should be made to the Electoral Claims Unit.

For by-elections in local councils, informal agreements are often arrived at so that sitting councillors resign to facilitate a by-election to coincide with the date of ordinary elections in May. This is more difficult to achieve when members die but parties have been known to delay requisitions so as to enable a May by-election. Thus, triple election commitments are reasonably common now – many two-tier areas have members that serve on both County and District Councils, possibly with town/parish membership too.

Printing ballots – different colours

In practical terms, this means dealing with three sets of ballot papers at the polling station and printing on different coloured paper six sets of ballots (tendered votes). All the papers must be of a different colour, which can be challenging for most administrators who wish to avoid using colours with traditional political connotations. Therefore, colours such as lilac, lime, puce, buff, etc. are pressed into service. The "primary" (usually parliamentary) elections ballot will traditionally be white and, after that, the key point is to avoid colours that look similar. This can get very complex because, at the count, with high-level fluorescent lighting in a sports hall, white and grey can appear similar. Another important consideration is whether or not the colour of the paper disadvantages those with poor or impaired vision, particularly bearing in mind that the lighting in some polling stations is poor. Cricket pavilion lighting is not designed for night use for elderly people reading, say, 20 names (some similar too) on a lengthy ballot paper which is one of three.

Obviously, early consultation with the printer is important in these circumstances so that suitable colours can be chosen and enough time gained to be able to print satisfactorily. Notices also have to be printed to be fitted into each voting compartment to indicate the relevant colour of each ballot paper, as well as advising of the maximum number of candidates that may be voted for.

One box or two?

This oft-asked question produces a variety of answers and practice throughout the country. Where it is possible to choose, they are clear pros and cons with both methods. Two boxes should be easier to handle at the count as the correct papers can easily be brought together quickly, avoiding time-consuming sorting and separating of ballots. However, that theory only works if the electors put the correct papers in the right boxes (not all read the signs on the boxes) – it only takes one ballot in the wrong box to throw out verification numbers and oblige the other box to be opened to search for the missing paper. Many people fold their papers together, some students (at some of the world's leading universities) think it both clever and amusing to take their ballots (or at least one) out of the polling station to adorn their bedsit wall... None of this makes the process any easier and it is unreasonable to expect polling station staff to watch every ballot going into the boxes, checking the correctness of the process. Indeed, at busy stations this can cause delay and deflects Presiding Officers from other duties. It is for these reasons that many Returning Officers simply use one box and go through the separation process at the count. It does take time and agents can get irritated at the apparent lack of progress.

It must be fairly recorded that other Returning Officers take an opposite view and think the two box method does work. Some stations do not produce discrepancies and, even if they do, it is claimed that it does not take long to open the other box to find the missing paper(s). This is all a matter of local custom and practice, reflecting different views throughout the country.

Issuing ballot papers

Whatever practice is followed, it is worthwhile giving some specific instruction to polling stations on ballot paper issuing, especially for the busy stations where there is a rush at a certain time. For these stations, it is worthwhile appointing some of the more experienced staff who are used to issuing papers while there are 30 or 40 people waiting. A calm but firm approach is called for along the lines of "I am issuing three ballots to you..." (assuming eligibility) rather than a vague and hopeless discussion about "...which colours would you like..." Voters cannot be forced to take all the ballots but they are perfectly entitled to put them into the box without making a choice – regrettably common in the case of combined polls where there is a parish or community council election with mainly independent candidates. If they wish to refuse a paper then so be it, but instruct staff to mark the register accordingly as they may return later in the day to exercise that vote. It is not up to the Presiding Officer to give lectures on the rightness (or wrongness) of all this (as has unfortunately been known), but simply to issue the ballots and ensure they are put in the box.

Of course, boxes do fill up more quickly and so spare boxes should be available, technically already sealed at 7.00am at the station ready for use – although it must be said that taking extra boxes into a particularly busy station in the evening is not too rare.

Postal votes – issue and return

The received wisdom for Electoral Administrators is that combined issue is more advantageous than separate issue. This is especially so now with one-piece mailers and where the electoral areas are wholly within one local authority; there are savings on manpower, paperwork and postal costs. The colour of respective ballot papers must be referred to in the postal voting instructions. Again, errors have been made in recent County Council electoral divisions where for the first time more than one member is being returned. The instructions on the one-piece mailer have traditionally been to vote for no more than one candidate for county elections, but with the correct "vote for up to two or three" (as applicable) on the ballot paper. It has been known for correction letters to have to be urgently sent to all recipients of postal votes in certain divisions after this printing error has been spotted following much unfavourable publicity in the local media, together with offers to replace so-called "spoilt" ballots already returned under this misapprehension. More usual instructions now advise to follow the instruction printed on each ballot paper.

Returning the postal votes to polling stations can cause some confusion. The statutory rule for combined issue is that votes can only be returned to those polling stations in the appropriate electoral area, i.e. parish postal must go back to the polling station within that parish. For an uncombined issue, the formal position is that a parliamentary ballot could go back to any polling station within that constituency but those for the district election could only be delivered to the polling stations within that district ward. Some would observe that such formal rules are not necessarily slavishly followed in practice – all postal votes (and they can be collected in during the day) get back to the count and are processed accordingly...clearly in the interests of democracy...

Agents at combined counts

The formal legal position is that, for combined polls, all the counting agents appointed for all elections have the right to scrutinise the separation of papers and consequent verification. However, only the counting agents appointed for a particular election can attend the counting of those votes and not those for another election for which they are not appointed.

Many Returning Officers/Electoral Administrators regard these particular rules as being especially petty and difficult to administer. In practice, many counting agents are dual/triple appointments (it is not so popular!) and, in any event, if the hall is large enough, democracy is better served by accountability, not apparent mean-spiritedness, even if backed by statute. In recent years, the Electoral Commission have received complaints from some of the national parties upon their agents being excluded from part of the count (even being obliged to stand outside the counting hall in inclement weather, which does seem over-zealous), though some Returning Officers/Electoral Administrators cite safety and limits on numbers in particular halls – yet another joy of combination!

Chapter 16

SOME CONCLUDING THOUGHTS

"There are two things which I am confident I can do very
well: one is an introduction to any literary work, stating
what it is to contain and how it should be executed in the
most perfect manner; the other is a conclusion, shewing
from various causes why the execution has not been equal
to what the author promised to himself and to the public"
Dr Johnson, writing in 1755

Old legislation, new problems

There are several references in this book to our outdated Victorian legislation, which is the framework for electoral law and practice; indeed, the text (whether satisfying Dr Johnson's tests or not) constantly documents the ensuing problems that are created by this legislative framework. Notwithstanding the well-documented issues, one of the great charms (if that be the correct word) of this situation is the ability of this venerable legislation to interact with other statutory provisions to create new and more testing conundrums. A good example of this occurred in the late summer/early autumn of 2007.

At that time, there was much media speculation as to the Prime Minister calling a General Election in early November. An issue that arose (and was picked up by the national media) was the state of the electoral register if an election was to be held at that time. That is the annual canvass period with Electoral Registration Officers distributing and collecting in their canvass forms to publish an updated, revised register on 1st December. The law provides that no monthly alterations are made during the canvass period. Of course, people are still moving house at this time; moreover, many students are leaving their home to pursue their studies elsewhere in the country and so large numbers are traditionally registered at their place of study. All this produces a "churn" effect on the register, with names moving on and off in various places. However, the outdated (August) register would not reflect these changes and they would not be captured until December publication of the revised register (October 15th is the reference date used for people to state their address). However, the new 2006 Act introduced a provision whereby it is possible to register anew, via a rolling registration form, if this is sent in to the appropriate Electoral Registration Officer before the eleventh working day prior to the poll. This provision, then, could catch the newly-arrived students and recent house movers.

The Electoral Commission issued advice to this effect (Circular 32/2007) but those administering registration and elections did both protest and express concern as to the practical application of this advice. To try to check thousands of canvass forms in the run-up to a General Election (a pretty busy period in any electoral office), identify those with changes and send to those so identified a pre-printed rolling registration form for speedy return seemed an immense task, bordering on the impossible. The whole scenario was compounded by postal strikes, as well as many electoral staff pointing out the difficulty of checking huge numbers of returned forms for accuracy and veracity: fraudulent registration is an issue in several locations and staff working under this pressure will make mistakes.

The arguments rumbled on in both public and private; the author pointed out on the BBC that the real answer was new legislation but continued that the remoteness of this simply increased logarithmically because Parliament was in recess at that time – just following the Party Conference season. The consensus view was that an election could be run but that probably about one million (and up to two million with a pessimistic view) would be disenfranchised. Ministry of Justice staff were in no doubts as to the problem and the fact that it would simply compound existing difficulties with software and printing. The actual extent of ministerial knowledge about the issue is difficult to quantify, but when eventually the Prime Minister announced there would be no election, a reference was made to "the register problem".

And so the issue rests there. Whether it will be revisited or resolved in the near future remains to be seen. However, if nothing is done and another autumn General Election is contemplated, the same difficulties will surely arise...

Caledonian considerations

Considerable and well-publicised problems were experienced in Scotland in May 2007 during their parliamentary and local elections ("Britain's biggest election scandal" according to the *Times*, apparently replacing the Birmingham case): exceptional number of rejected ballots, problems over combination of polls, delays in announcing results with overnight counts and recounts, etc. The current text will not rehearse all the Review findings (written by the Canadian, Ron Gould) in the report commissioned by the Electoral Commission (published October 2007) but a number of key points are highly instructive, of great contemporary relevance and most are surely applicable south of the border too:

- Electoral legislation needs to be rationalised and consolidated.

- A chief Returning Officer for Scotland should be appointed to be responsible for overseeing Scottish Parliamentary and local elections (a similar post already exists for Northern Ireland).

- Combined elections are a disservice to local government and its candidates. Separate elections better enable voters to engage with the campaign in a meaningful way and make a knowledgeable decision.

- There should be timetable changes in that the provisions for postal voting do not allow sufficient time for printing the ballot papers following the close of nominations. The report recommends the close of nominations should be 23 days before polling day rather than 16. The final day for postal vote applications should also be set earlier.

● As polling now ceases at 10.00pm, there should be no overnight counts.

The foregoing (containing changes that would be welcomed by English electoral administrators?) is only a selection of the main points but, if such steps are implemented by the Scottish Government, there would be even more variety within UK electoral systems.

Performance management

Another new and significant development has been the introduction of performance indicators by the Electoral Commission to set standards in electoral registration – accuracy and coverage of registers, etc. This is ongoing into 2008 but it seems inevitable that further standards will be introduced to cover other aspects of electoral work. The Commission gained these powers from the 2006 Electoral Administration Act but, whatever their merits, their timing is more than a little unfortunate. They were announced in October 2007, only four days after the CLG published a new skimmed-down overall performance framework for local government of 198 indicators (daunting enough!).

No doubt the Commission is well meaning in its desire to improve registration work but, for many in local government, this does seem to be a backward step in trying to micro-manage local performance. Speaking at the 2007 SOLACE conference, Hazel Blears, the Department for Communities and Local Government Secretary of State, said that she would guard against the position of extra targets "through the back door". The real issue here, of course, is the unjoined-up nature of Whitehall with its various unconnected bodies and Central Government Departments. The Ministry of Justice and the Electoral Commission clearly have a working relationship, but the awareness of CLG of this is clearly questionable. It must be clearly recorded, however, that representations were made to the Commission by local authority Chief Executives who tried to point out the dismantling of the detailed performance target regime.

For administrators there will be a further new burden of work, but will any of this improve registration? More to the point, will it attract further resources in areas of need? These will remain key questions that have to be answered in the future.

And finally...

These concluding thoughts simply show that, although there are changes afoot in the electoral world, there is certainly no overall master plan with key goals for the future. Major new or consolidating legislation seems unlikely in the short to medium term and Central Government will continue with new initiatives (weekend polls and voting at 16 are rumoured now to be popular) as well as tinkering with the existing rules. None of this makes for an easier life for those that administer elections but, to be positive, the resilience and skill of such people is simply exemplary and it is for that reason alone that elections will continue to be run with a substantial measure of success in this country.

INDEX